W9-BNP-051

KISS
YOURSELF
—AND—
HUG
—THE—
WORLD

KISS
YOURSELF
AND
HUG
THE
WORLD

*Keys to Authentic
and Vital Living*

GEORGE F. REGAS

WORD BOOKS
PUBLISHER
WACO, TEXAS
A DIVISION OF
WORD, INCORPORATED

Unless otherwise indicated, Scripture quotations are from The New English Bible (NEB), Copyright © The Delegates of the Oxford University Press and The Syndics of the Cambridge University Press, 1961, 1970. Reprinted by permission.

Other Scripture quotations are from the following sources:
The King James Version of the Bible (KJV).
The New King James Version (NKJV). Copyright © 1979, 1980, 1982, Thomas Nelson, Inc., Publishers.
The Revised Standard Version of the Bible (RSV), copyrighted 1946, 1952, © 1971, 1973 by the Division of Christian Education of the National Council of the Churches of Christ in the U.S.A., used by permission.
The New Testament in Modern English (PHILLIPS) by J. B. Phillips, published by The Macmillan Company, © 1958, 1960, 1972 by J. B. Phillips.

Library of Congress Cataloging-in-Publication Data:
Regas, George, 1930–
Kiss yourself and hug the world.

1. Christian life—Anglican authors.   I. Title.
BV4501.2.R424 1987   248.4'83   87-15986
ISBN 0-8499-0391-2

Printed in the United States of America

7 8 9 8   RRD 9 8 7 6 5 4 3 2 1

To All Saints Church, Pasadena, California—
an incredible, beautiful, life-filled community where I have served
as a priest for twenty years. We have been
companions on an exciting journey.

Contents

Acknowledgments

This book would have been impossible without the careful collaboration of my executive assistant, Anne Breck Peterson. For nine years she has enriched my ministry. In the midst of an enormously demanding schedule, she has helped make my professional life work so that this book could be written.

I am indebted to my secretary of ten years, Lois Marski, for her graceful, patient, and skillful work in typing and retyping and retyping the manuscript!

Many years ago, Floyd Thatcher, Editor-in-Chief of Word Books, saw a book in me and persisted in urging me to put it on paper. I know the essential role he played in this, my first book, and I am grateful. My careful editor, Anne Christian Buchanan, has played a valuable part in seeing this project reach completion. I acknowledge this with thanks.

I have been given such incredible, loving support by Mary, my wife; her graceful encouragement made me believe a book was possible. And all that wonderful family of mine—Michelle and Tom, Susan and Bo, Tim and Tyler, Burke and Lowry, and Nicholas—have loved and nurtured me on my journey. Had they not given me lots of understanding, grace, patience, and laughter over the years, this book would never have made it to the publisher. Thanks and love.

GEORGE F. REGAS

Introduction

I love that eighteenth-century inscription on the tomb of the Countess of Huntington just outside Winchester, England: "She was a just, godly, righteous and sober lady, bounteous in good works and Christian affections, a firm believer in the Gospel of our Lord and Savior Jesus Christ, and devoid of the taint of enthusiasm."

Few today would prize a life "devoid of enthusiasm." We want to feel life deeply and live it passionately. However, we live in an environment which from the beginning of life tells us there is a pill we can take to make all the hurting in life stop. In essence, we are promised a pain-free life, and we go to great lengths to obtain it—even if doing so means deadening our feelings, masking them, flattening them.

We'll do anything to take away those agonizing hurts of life. But the cost is high. For feeling no pain means we no longer feel deeply about anything. So there is no vitality, no vigor, no passion in our lives. And for that we suffer greatly.

It is a supreme personal victory when we truly feel for people, when we are willing to take the risks of loving another person even with the possibility that we may be hurt. But many of us are so fearful of the hurts of disappointment that we are willing to deaden our feelings and forego the possibilities of vital, loving, joyful, passionate life.

We come alive when we allow ourselves to feel the pain and the joy of another person, to experience *compassion.* The apostle Paul gives us a definition of this virtue: "Love in all sincerity . . . with the joyful be joyful, and mourn with the mourners" (Rom. 12:9, 15).

Compassion—"suffering with" is the actual definition of the word—is that quality of imaginatively projecting our life into the life of another so that we are able to feel for that person and are moved to alleviate some of the pain and distress of his or her life. Compassion means tying our

11

sensitivities to our neighbor's nerve endings and feeling things as he does. It means getting under the other person's skin and experiencing life as she does. It means endeavoring to look at the world through his eyes and to comprehend the reasons he is doing what he does.

I have been told that it is rather easy to tap a person's telephone and hear all that goes on in conversations. Compassion is that quality of life that presupposes the imaginative power necessary to tap in on what the other person is saying inside. It tunes in on her aspirations, her joys and pains, her hopes and terrors, her shame and longing.

Compassion is that deep feeling within us that desires to share the joys and the pains of another person and by that sharing to help transform life.

Do we really care about other people? That is a bedrock question of life. Obviously there are pockets of magnificent caring and compassion here and there throughout America. But I worry about what is happening to our society at large.

In the twentieth century, we've made unbelievable strides in the acquisition of knowledge. There seems to be no end to what exploring minds can do; no scientific problem seems to be beyond us. The scientific progress made in medicine in the last twenty-five years staggers the mind. The technical skills involved in penetrating the vast reaches of space are incomprehensible to most of us.

I rejoice in this pursuit of knowledge, for brain power will be needed to save this shattered earth, to heal its wounds, to create order out of chaos. What concerns me is how frequently all this knowledge is divorced from feeling. Our minds are full of information, but, as Ezekiel said, we have hearts of stone.

I once heard Helen Caldicott, former president of Physicians for Social Responsibility and a tireless campaigner for a world free of nuclear fear, tell of an interview in which she had spoken of the peril the children of the world had been placed in by the escalating arms race. During the interview, her voice shook with emotion and she came close to tears. Afterwards the interviewer was critical of this behavior, asking if she weren't letting her emotions carry her away about a complex issue that clearly demanded keen, rational thought.

Dr. Caldicott shot back that nothing was more important in all of life than preserving the earth for our children! As a mother, a physician, and a human being, she was passionate about the need to say this—and to act on her beliefs. She went on to say that what was needed to save the world were more clear heads fired up by passionate hearts.

And that is exactly what we need to live full, meaningful lives. We need passion in the mind—that is to say, we need to feel deeply what we know. For without this caring deeply, feeling passionately about what we know, we live incomplete, truncated lives.

We are so overwhelmed and stunned by the oppressive number of facts about what is happening in our world. Everywhere the facts bear down on us: the despair of the hungry, the anguish of the poor, the desolation of the homeless, the hatred between races and religions and nations, the ever-increasing stockpile of nuclear weapons, the almost unstoppable supply of illegal drugs that affects every segment of society.

In Los Angeles County, where I live, there were thirty-five thousand homeless people in 1987—and we have only a hundred shelters with thirty-six hundred beds to alleviate this need. We have an estimated two thousand to ten thousand runaway teenagers roaming our streets, but there are only fifty-nine beds in all of the county to help these desperate children. Our failure here is not a lack of knowledge, an absence of facts. Our failure is that we do not feel what we know. That is the flaw at the heart of our nation, and it could lead to our ruin.

When we inject ourselves with spiritual novocaine and deaden ourselves to feeling the pain and anguish of the world, we pay an enormous price. We miss out on vital, vigorous, passionate living. We turn off the misery of the poor, those casualties of our economic system, and then wonder why our hearts feel so dead and our souls so numb!

If we are to make our way into passionate living, into a life that is full, vigorous, and authentic, then we need to get a firm grasp on the interconnectedness of all life. The University of

Chicago theologian Joseph Sittler uses the provocative image of a spider web to convey this fact. Touch one part of it and all parts quiver.

That's the way it is with our feelings. We bring to life one dimension of our emotions, and our whole being is raised to emotional vitality. But we deaden one part of our feeling personalities, and most everything else goes numb.

I think we can see this principle clearly in the area of sexual love. The curious thing about the ferment of the sexual revolution of the last twenty-five years is how little men and women seem to be enjoying their emancipation as they go from partner to partner. There is lots of sex but, the research indicates, not much joy, not much passion, not much deep feeling.

For a number of years *The Joy of Sex* was a number-one bestseller in America. I was basically happy about that because I believe lovers should increase their adequacy and enjoyment of the wonderful experience of sexual love by being armed with adequate information. However, the great psychoanalyst, Rollo May, in *Love and Will*,[1] makes an interesting point about the recent emphasis on learning the art of sexual love. Dr. May says there is an inverse relationship between the number of how-to-do-it books rolling off the presses and the amount of sexual passion and pleasure experienced by the people involved!

I would say this might indicate there is a direct relation between compassion and passion. Our emotions are interconnected. If the power to feel and suffer with another person is thwarted; if the power to care about the children in El Salvador, Nicaragua, and Lebanon, so mangled by the tragedy of war, has dried up and we no longer cry for them; if we have suppressed this emotion of feeling the pains of the world's sick and starving people because it is all so overwhelming; if our hearts are not broken when the vicious system of apartheid in South Africa breaks the hearts of young people who aspire to be somebody in this world; if we cannot put ourselves inside our lover's heart so that we feel the fears and hopes and joys and pains of her heart; if apathy reigns in our bodies—then the result of this erosion of compassion, this shot of spiritual novocaine to numb our feelings, is that we will have serious trouble having any passionate and ecstatic feelings in the most intimate act of sexual love.

That impoverishment will send many out into the eroticism of the sexual wilderness, desperately searching but never finding passion. Some people seem to think they can simplify sex and treat it like a combination of learning to play tennis and buying life insurance!

The older I grow, the more convinced I am that passion—the deepest, strongest, most alive feeling—is linked with compassion. Maybe the greatest lovers are those who care deeply about the pain and agony of their brothers and sisters of the world, who choose to bear some of those burdens and transform the pain.

As we come to enjoy fully the wonder and beauty and glory and loveliness of life, and as we also take into our hearts some of the burden of pain which lies upon the world—then we are on our way in the search for passionate and authentic living. The world might think it absurd, but Christians have a way of believing that if we give our lives away for the healing of the world, happiness and joy and fullness of life will come along in the parentheses.

Both of these concepts make up the basic thrust of this book. An enthusiastic enjoyment of the earth's richness and an active participation in making the world a more livable, beautiful, peace-filled place—both are part of the Jewish Christian heritage; both are part of the human struggle for passionate, authentic life.

E. B. White put it wonderfully: "If the world were merely seductive, that would be easy. If it were merely challenging, that would be no problem. But if I arise in the morning torn between a desire to improve the world and a desire to enjoy the world, this makes it hard to plan the day."

The intent of this book is to help you plan the day. It is a book about joy in a desperate world, love in the midst of a violent culture, hope when all the lights of the world go out. It is a book about living deeply and fully. It is a book about passionate and authentic living.

Part One

The Basics for Passionate Living

Chapter One

Trust: The Essential Element for Survival

Some years ago *Time* magazine reported on a nervous motorist in Lambertville, New Jersey. This man, on being stopped by the police, explained that he had been driving on two hundred and twenty-four consecutive learner's permits over the last twenty-five years. He had flunked his first driver's test and had been unsure of himself ever since! What a modern parable for the insecurity and uncertainty of our age.

The values that guide us are not clear any more. Cyclonic change bewilders us. Even the two trillion dollars we've spent on military arms since 1945 have produced sophisticated weaponry which in its nuclear capacity is as much a threat to us as to our enemy. The money spent for security has not made us feel secure. The foundations on which we stand don't appear to be very solid.

But we long for solid foundations; we want something that will make us utterly secure. Like Captain Ahab in *Moby Dick,* "We need to feel something in this slippery world that can hold."

We have such a deep desire for certainty that part of us is tempted to buy into a brand of religion that claims to have all the answers to those baffling questions about contemporary life—a variety of religion that is neatly and securely packaged.

Often I listen on my car radio to preachers who seem to have all the answers. And while I sometimes think their material is untenable, I can understand their appeal. In fact, the overwhelming certitude with which they deal with every issue has an almost physical effect upon me, and I sometimes wish

I could relax and be carried by those simple, certain answers to life's complexities.

But I resist that temptation fiercely. The healthier and wiser part of me knows that the pursuit of certitude is not a genuinely religious pursuit; rather, it is a corruption of religion. The arrogance of conviction is not creative, whether from the lips of a liberal politician or a conservative one, whether from a theologian or an economist. "I've got the answer, and I'll give it to you with absolute finality." Run when you hear that! It can never lead to healthy life or creative faith.

Not only do we seek all the right answers; we have an almost insatiable desire to have control of life—control of things, of people, of God. Former Secretary of State Alexander Haig, his voice trembling after the assassination attempt on President Reagan in 1982, said, "I am in control"—almost as if saying it would make it so. In a deeper sense, that is what we all are tempted to say. However, that is not the authentic religious posture. The Christian faith calls for a decision to trust, and you trust only what you cannot control.

Some of us know how this works in a human relationship. We want to be in control and make certain that a particular person belongs to us in the ways we think appropriate. But such a grip of control constricts the flow of life in a relationship. Only when we trust a person because we believe in her and are willing to place ourselves vulnerably in an uncontrolling relationship does that relationship come alive and flourish.

So it is with God. Our relationship with God dwindles and dies when we try to replace trust with security. That fact is basic to all we know about vital, passionate living.

I

Nowhere in human history is the life of daring trust more clearly revealed than in the crucifixion of Jesus.

It would be impossible to exaggerate the horror, the shame, the humiliation, the loneliness of the last twelve hours leading up to Jesus' crucifixion.

A bloodthirsty mob took Jesus outside the walls of Jerusalem to a low hill shaped like a skull. And there they laid him down on two pieces of wood and stretched his arms along the crossbeams. A nail was driven through the palm of each hand to hold him there. His feet were nailed one over the other to the upright pole. Then, in a moment of searing agony, they raised the cross and put it in its socket.

In the dark bleakness of the final hour, Jesus' lonely, pain-drenched figure uttered a cry of desolation which even now makes the heart stand still: "My God, my God, why have you forsaken me?" (Mark 15:34, NKJV).

The mystery of those words lies beyond my understanding. Yet I believe that this moment of torment and despair in Jesus' soul is central to the passion and death of Jesus.

On the cross Jesus had been magnificent, reaching out in love to the very ones who had lashed his back and nailed him to the hard wood of the cross. He had prayed for the soldiers and spectators, listened to the two criminals on the cross beside him, and saved one from his dread of the future.

He had looked out for everyone else. Now it seemed that no one was looking out for him. Not even God.

It seemed as if the bottom of life itself had dropped out. Everything beautiful and divine seemed so distant. Good people had disappeared, and coarseness and violence and brutality and anger seemed to have won the day. So Jesus shrieked, "My God, my God, why have you forsaken me?"

At that moment Jesus is very close to us. For how many of us have been spared those feelings? It is all right to doubt. It is all right to be angry with God. It is all right to cry when the lights of our world go out.

Unamuno wrote, years ago, that the proper use of a temple or church is as a place where people go to weep in common, to grieve together.

And how we grieve. Things we've believed in and trusted all our lives let us down. The lights go out in our world.

A son goes through college and is ready for a good career. His parents are proud. Then the Vietnam war breaks out and he goes off to battle and is killed.

A woman gives her love—her heart and soul and body—to a man, believing they have a rich future together. He lets her down, walks away without even a tear. Now she wonders if she should risk a vulnerable involvement again.

We believe profoundly in some friends and they betray us, hurt us deeply.

We work hard on our careers, with high aspirations for great achievement, and are given a bad deal. And we are bitter and resentful.

We are happy, and life goes beautifully for us. Then the death of a loved one shocks us. The duties of life numb us. Life's meaning is eroded.

We do feel close to a Jesus who on the cross feels everything is gone and the story of his ministry is about to be blasted away. And so we cry as he cries, "My God, my God, why have you forsaken me?"

II

But that isn't all we see in Jesus on the cross.

There were many unanswered questions in Jesus' heart when he came to the end. Life's puzzle still baffled him. Yet underneath what appeared to be defeat and failure was a curious note of victory.

True, the cry of despair was there. But it was not the last word from the cross. Don't ever forget that Jesus' last words were those of a prayer he had learned as a little boy and said all his life: "Father, into Your hands I commit my spirit" (Luke 23:46, NKJV).

In his book, *The Sacred Journey,* Frederick Buechner tells of a piece of art that has had enormous influence in his life. "It is a pastel of the head of Jesus that Leonardo da Vinci did as a study for the Last Supper. The head is tipped slightly to one side and down," writes Buechner. "He looks Jewish. He looks very tired. Some of the color has flaked away. His eyes are closed.

"That was the face," says Buechner, "that moved me and stayed with me more in a way than all the others, though not because it was Jesus' face, as far as I can remember, but just because it seemed the face of a human being to whom everything had happened that can happen. It was a face of a great stillness, a face that had survived."[1]

That is the Jesus I see on the cross. That is the suffering figure that has riveted the attention of people over the centuries in their most tragic hours.

With life bleak as hell, with most of those he loved in desertion, with the mob screaming words of hatred and ridicule, Jesus still trusted in the ultimate goodness of his God; he still trusted that God's hand would hold him and that somehow, someway, God would make something good of his death.

Who is really the person of faith? Someone who can believe in all the miracles in the Bible? Someone who can swallow more dogma than the next person? Or someone like Alice in Wonderland, who attempted to believe ten impossible things each day before breakfast?

I doubt it. Rather, the person of faith is the one who trusts that at the center and heart of all things is a creative power on the side of what is good and just and loving.

The person of faith is the one who decides to live as if God's universe were ultimately on the side of goodness, truth, and beauty.

Anne Frank was a person who had that kind of faith. She was a courageous young Jewish girl who hid with her family in an attic to escape the Nazis, but who was finally caught and sent to her death. Her diary from those dark years of hiding has been preserved, and the words from that diary still inspire me: "In spite of everything, life is good."

III

In his cry of despair at feeling deserted and in his prayer of trust as he commits himself into God's hands, Jesus points the way to authentic, healthy faith.

In people's heart-wrenching hours of grief and loneliness, they cry out, "My God, my God, why?" The explanations of why there is suffering in the world, the answers to the unfairness of life's tragedies are unknown to us. What is the satisfactory theory on what God was doing as six million Jews were led to the gas ovens? The "why" of that monstrous horror is unknown.

Yet our deepest need is not for explanation of *why* a tragic thing has happened, but rather of *how* we are to face it and gain a victory. And the answer to that "how" is to be able to trust God to be with us in the darkest hell.

One thing this cross of Jesus proclaims to us is that God is there in the bleak darkness. An impressive picture hangs in the National Gallery in London. Christ is on the cross, almost hidden in the darkness. At first, the one who looks at the painting observes nothing but the bleakness, and through it the dim figure of the Savior. But if you look more closely, you discern a figure with arms outstretched, tenderly holding up the suffering one. God's face is twisted by a pain which is more agonizing even than that of the Christ. God is grieving with God's son as he hangs on the cross. God's heart is crushed when the son's heart is broken. That is the only vista I can see that gives us some clue to the impossible questions on suffering.

"Father, into your hands I commit my spirit."

In that prayer he had said all his life, Jesus was affirming the trust that God would hold safe what was committed to God. In that prayer, he was joining himself to a love that was stronger than death, and binding his life to the creative energy of the universe which can bring good out of every defeat.

God suffers with us. I do know that in my bleakest hours, in the pit of my miniature hells, I have felt the presence of God. God goes through the valley with you and me. That is our only hope when the lights go out. And I've seen people who, facing the worst that life could bring, still trusted in the goodness of God. They are glorious people.

IV

If you are to have health and vitality in your life, you must make a decision. Will you trust the promises of God that God will never leave you, never desert you?

We all want life to be beautiful and rich and fulfilling. But if the day comes when all the lights go out and all your supports are ripped loose, will you trust God's promises that God will be there in spite of everything? God can bring good out of suffering if you love and trust God.

I've seen the greatest living come out of such trust. It takes a lot of courage to reach out across the boundaries of finitude and grasp a hand that will hold you forever. But it is a courage that sets you free from fear and fills you with peace.

There is a poignant story of a young husband whose wife died and left him with a small son. Back home after the funeral, they went to bed as soon as dark came because there was nothing else the father could think of that he could bear to do.

As they lay there in the darkness, numb with sorrow, the little boy broke the stillness from his bed with disturbing questions. "Daddy, where is mommy?" The father tried to get the boy to sleep, but the questions kept coming from his sad, childish mind.

After a time the father got up and brought the little boy to bed with him. But the child was still disturbed and restless and would occasionally ask probing, heartbreaking questions. Finally the youngster reached a hand through the darkness, placed it on his father's face, and asked, "Daddy, is your face toward me?" Given assurance, verbally and by his own touch, that his father's face was toward him, the boy said, "If your face is toward me, I think I can go to sleep."

In this dark, confusing, troubling world, I believe God is saying to us through the cross of Jesus, "My face is toward you, my son, my daughter. Be at peace."

Will you trust that? It can change your life forever.

Chapter Two

Hope: A Passion for
Life's Possibilities

Incredible things happen when people anchor their lives in hope. They release into their being power to do what appears to be impossible. As Norman Cousins says, "We must recognize that we get our basic energy not from turbines but from hope."

In the bleakest moments of World War II, Maximilian Kolbe, a Polish Franciscan priest, refused to give way to despair. He kept on believing that goodness would somehow prevail over the monstrosities of Hitler.

That courageous hope marked his life at Auschwitz, where he was imprisoned for his opposition to the Nazis. And it shone most clearly the day that the German commander of Auschwitz ordered ten prisoners to die by starvation as a reprisal for the escape of one inmate. The grisly quota was arbitrarily filled, and one of the victims, Gajowniczek, a Polish army sergeant, began to sob, "My wife and my children . . my wife and my children."

Suddenly Kolbe pushed his way from the back of the formation to the front, past the security guards, right to the commander and looked him straight in the eye.

"I wish to make a request, please," he said in impeccable German.

"What do you want?"

"I want to die in the place of this prisoner," answered Fr. Kolbe, pointing to the sobbing man, Gajowniczek. "I have no wife and no children. Besides, I'm old and cannot do much good anymore."

The stunned prisoners waited for the Germans to say both men would die. But after a moment the commander snapped, "Request granted."

So Maximilian Kolbe gave his life for another, and that courageous act brought light into the midst of the blackest hell. Hope had released in him the power to face death and to believe goodness and justice would ultimately triumph.

And in October of 1982, in St. Peter's Basilica in Rome, Pope John Paul II canonized Maximilian Kolbe a saint in the Roman Catholic Church because through prosperity and loss, through high moments and the experiences of the valley, through good report and evil report, through light and darkness he remained hopeful. And from that hope came forth a courageous and radiant spirit.

Patricia Treece, his biographer, says that this invincible hope was central to Kolbe's life. He never quit believing that beauty and love and kindness would somehow prevail. The life of Maximilian Kolbe bears the authentic marks of the kind of person of God described in the Epistle to the Hebrews: "Christ is faithful as a son, set over his household. And we are that household of his, if only we are fearless and keep our hope high" (Heb. 3:6).

Hope does not seem to be in large supply in our society. Pollster George Gallup says, "There has never been a time in the forty years that we have been conducting our surveys that we have found the population to be so pessimistic." We might identify less with Maximilian Kolbe and more with the characters in that crazy story of the man about to jump off the Brooklyn Bridge. Held back by a policeman, the desperate man showed the officer the headlines of the morning newspaper he had been reading. Then they both jumped.

Recently I saw a production of Marsha Norman's Pulitzer Prize winning play, *'Night, Mother*. It is a devastating, soul-wrenching play about a mother and her grown daughter. And it is filled with pain and defeat. Jessie, the young woman, looks out at the world and sees disappointment in the woman she has become, in her family, in the world around her. She methodically plans her suicide, talks it through with her mother, and achieves it.

In one of the last struggling conversations between the two, Jessie's mother tries to say life will be better. Jessie responds that her suicide is her way of looking at life and all the people, and saying no to all of it. Almost screaming, Jessie adds, "Mamma, I say no to hope!" And then she goes into her bedroom and locks the door—and we hear the shot.

About the same time I finished reading Maya Angelou's magnificent book, *All God's Children Need Traveling Shoes,* in which she relates how she joined a colony of black American expatriates in Ghana.

She closes with a reflection on all the grief and pain blacks have endured over the centuries. She says she wept as she thought of the past—but with a curious joy. These are Angelou's words:

> Despite the murders, rapes, and suicides, we had survived.
> . . . The auction block had not erased us. Not humiliations or lynchings, individual cruelties nor collective oppression had been able to eradicate us from the earth. We had come through despite our ignorances and gullibility and the ignorances and rapacious greed of our assailants. . . . There was much to cry for, much to mourn, but in my heart I felt exalted knowing there was much to celebrate. . . . Through the centuries of despair and dislocation, we had been creative, *because we faced down death by daring to hope.*[1]

As I've pondered the basics for a passionate, vital life, the voices of those two women have been echoing in the chamber of my mind. For what the hope-filled Maya and the hopeless Jessie are really saying—one in a positive and one in a negative way—is that hope and life cannot be separated. For suicide is the logical result of a hopeless life. But when we dare to hope—and realistic hope does take courage—we say yes to life, and in so doing we can face down even death.

Cicero's famous maxim, "While there is life there is hope," tells an even greater truth when it is reversed: "Where there is hope there is life."

And so at the heart of the Christian life is this challenge to choose life by daring to hope: "We are the household of God, if only we are fearless and keep our hope high."

I

To lose hope is a calamity. It is a devastating day for the human race if we lose the driving power of our hope to build a new world of love with justice. And it is a terrible day in our lives if we let our defeats beat us down into cynicism and despair.

The failure of hope is total failure. Despair is the death-blow to civilization. It is unmistakably clear that when we lose our capacity to hope we lose our capacity to shape the future.

The deepest tragedies I see are those in which people have given up and no longer hope for a better, more wonderful day. Without hope, there is no real, authentic life possible.

But here is the positive side to that powerful truth: Hope is powerful enough to keep an entire race of people alive! As Maya Angelou says, "We face down death by daring to hope."

I am convinced that those who live in the healthiest and most authentic dimensions of life are those who have the courage to be dreamers of a better world and a more wonderful life—and say with their lives that such things are still possible.

Years ago, William Hazlitt wrote, "Man is the only animal that laughs and weeps, for he is the only animal struck with the difference between what things are and what they ought to be."

But hope takes us one step beyond laughter and tears, for hope gives us a vision of the difference between what things are and what they *might* be. To hope means to be grasped and claimed by the truth of life's incredible possibilities and with God's strength to move toward those dreams. It means we have a passion for those possibilities and are driven by grace toward their realization.

When this kind of hope fills our beings—a hope that life can be different, that life can be healed and transformed, that life can be better and more wonderful—when that audacious hope fills our hearts, there is released in us an incredible energy that moves us toward that new life in Christ. I can think of no higher task for a Christian church than to liberate people from their feeling of hopelessness. "We are the household of God, if only we are fearless and keep our hope high."

II

"Keep our hope high"—for only with courageous hope can we be the creators of that new world with peace and justice.

Isn't that the reason Martin Luther King, Jr.'s famous speech, "I Have A Dream," given on August 28, 1963 before the Lincoln Memorial, still resonates in us with such enormous power?:

> So I say to you, my friends, that even though we face the difficulties of today and tomorrow, I still have a dream. It is a dream deeply rooted in the American dream that one day this nation will rise up and live out the true meaning of its creed— "We hold these truths to be self-evident, that all men are created equal." . . .
>
> I have a dream my four little children will one day live in a nation where they will not be judged by the color of their skin but by the content of their character. I have a dream today! . . .
>
> This is our hope. This is the faith that I go back to the South with. With this faith we will be able to hew out of the mountain of despair a stone of hope. With this faith we will be able to transform the jangling discord of our nation into a beautiful symphony of brotherhood. With this faith we will be able to work together, to pray together, to struggle together . . . to stand up for freedom together, knowing that we will be free one day. . . . "Free at last! Free at last! Thank God Almighty, we are free at last."[1]

No matter how bleak life became, no matter how seemingly impossible were the aspirations for a new America where all people were treated with equality, Dr. King never lost hope. That was the driving power of his life and the sustaining force of the Civil Rights movement.

It is true that we live today with much of Dr. King's dream

unrealized. The *Los Angeles Times*, in a recent editorial, said, "Dr. King's description that blacks live on 'an island of poverty in the midst of a vast ocean of material prosperity, exiles in their own land' remains as valid for today as that day on which he said it."

Even a cursory look around confirms that assessment. For example, even though the general unemployment figures declined slightly in 1986, in the black community the issue of work remained a nightmare. There was 22% unemployment among blacks, and 45% of black youth were out of work.

God created all of us in God's image. That divine thumbprint on our souls means we, too, are to be workers and creators. The tragic scandal of unemployment is its dehumanization. America's dream is for all people to have the opportunity and dignity of work—and of being fully human.

That dream is deferred, but we keep on dreaming—and daring to hope. And we keep working to give light to King's bleak world, moved by those words of Teilhard de Chardin, the French theologian and scientist: "The world of tomorrow belongs to those who brought it greatest hope."

We will make our way to that America where all people have an equal chance to succeed when we believe it is possible and have a plan for that possibility.

Rabbi Leonard Beerman of Leo Baeck Temple in Los Angeles is a close friend with whom I have traveled throughout the world on missions of peace. These hope-filled words of his move me in the deepest places of my spirit: "Believing, in spite of everything, that the way to give meaning to life is to do what we can to abate its misery, to be among those who work to heal its wounds, to be comrades in the struggle to extend the domain of love and reconciliation and justice in the world. This has been our dream, a deep dream, of love and transformation. It is a good dream, my friends. Don't let anyone take it away from us."

We will have a new world when there are enough of us who, like Leonard Beerman, still have the courage to hope—when enough of us say with our lives that it is still possible to feed the hungry and shelter the homeless; to liberate those oppressed by racism, to find creative employment for everyone able to work; to care for the sick, especially the poor and elderly; to free the world from sexual prejudices and nationalistic arrogance; to preserve this fragile earth, our island home; to tame the savagery in humanity and make gentle the life of the earth; and to end war forever.

To believe such a world is still possible is a song of hope we must sing to ourselves and to our children. No gift to our children can compare to that of hope—that we have not given up on the future.

III

"Keep our hope high"—for it is the great force at work within you for the attainment of the life of wholeness you personally seek.

I know what despair and discouragement have done in my own life, what wreckage they create. But I have also experienced the healing power of hope and seen life rebuilt.

I've seen hope at work in so many lives around me that I could never doubt its power. I've seen people who lost hope die overnight, and I've seen people who kept hope alive endure the "tortures of the damned" and emerge physically and spiritually strong and beautiful.

Late one night I was called to the hospital. The doctor was a member of my parish and knew I had a close relationship with his patient, who had undergone serious surgery and then began running an unexpectedly high temperature.

The medical people could not find the cause for the fever, and the patient's condition grew worse. The physician was alarmed, for the patient's life was in jeopardy, and nothing the medical team tried seemed to help.

I spent several hours with my parishioner. Soon it became obvious that he was bottled up with fear and a deep despondency about his future. He had just experienced the soul-shattering event of his wife's divorcing him after thirty-five years of marriage. As we talked about his fears and his deep despair and his absence of real hope, he began to see how all these things were blocking the healing power of God in his life. So he agreed to let me try to help him in his hopelessness.

First, I asked him to picture in his mind the healthy person he prayed God would make him. What would he like to become with God's help?

And then I gave him that important verse from Hebrews to say over and over again through the night: "We are the household of God, if only we are fearless and keep our hope high!"

The next morning he was a new man on his way to health. Gradually, I could see hope transforming despair and trust taking the place of fear. "For we are saved by hope" (Rom. 8:24, KJV). Paul's words were literally true for my friend.

There is a fable about the devil's going out of business. Hate, lust, cruelty, possessiveness, apathy, vindictiveness— all were put up for sale and sold. One thing was left to the very last—for hopelessness had the highest price tag of all. When everything else had failed, the devil knew he could take despair and pry open our hearts, get down inside of us, and destroy us.

But if we have hope, nothing can stop us. Maya Angelou was right. "We faced down death by daring to hope." The most insistent plea of the spirit of God is to "keep your hope high."

IV

Hope is a very practical reality. Hope releases the energy in us for converting those intangible dreams into tangible realities.

Get hold of the idea of hope's immeasurable power. Something tremendous happens when we move out to make our life match our dreams, when we try to grasp our vision of life's possibilities. God is in that hope. And hope means energy.

When we reach across the chasm of estrangement and grasp the hand of our husband or wife for a new future, when we take one brave step toward bringing peace to this tortured and brutalized world, when we open the door of welcome to a son or daughter who has betrayed so many of the things we stand for, when we seek to have the dreams of life's possibilities fulfilled—God is with us. The very power of creation is released into our lives to sustain us. That's the miracle of hope.

Melancholia is a woodcutting by Albrecht Dürer in which a woman sits dejectedly on the ground before a city in need of restoration. Beside her is a box of tools—aids to her work in building a new city. But she appears to be hopelessly immobilized with her hands behind her. Without hope, she contributes nothing to life. Nothing seems possible, so nothing is attempted.

The eighteenth-century Irish statesman Edmund Burke said, "The only thing necessary for the triumph of evil is for good people to do nothing." Good people *will* do nothing if they have lost hope, if they are convinced by the chic pessimism of our day that there is nothing we can do to change life in this complex and baffling world.

Believe in miracles—believe hope can topple despair in the hearts of people. We need a miracle if we are to survive in our complicated age.

Our greatest problem has never been the absence of answers to difficult situations. Humanity's greatest problem has been the absence of the will to attack problems.

I believe it is hope that arouses the will to change life, and it is hope that strengthens and sustains us through the heat of the day.

Despair is part of the decadence of our age, for it saps our ethical sensitivities and our moral strength. The sturdy, persistent hope of the Bible is part of our vitality and our health. So the race is on between decadence and vitality, between despair and hope, between giving in to the old world of violence and creating a new earth of peace. Real faith is the fearless courage to put your life on the side of hope—the courage to live out a life trusting in the goodness of God and the ultimate triumph of God's purposes.

Chapter Three

Love: No Life Without It

One morning, many years ago, I was working in my study at home in New York when my younger daughter, then about five years old, opened the door and peeked in to see what I was doing. She knew she was interrupting me, but obviously enjoyed the fact. I can still see that grin on her face.

I sat back in my chair and called her to come in, indicating that I had a very *special secret* to tell her. She ran to me and I whispered in her ear, "I think you are a wonderful person." Susan stood back and said, "Oh, Daddy, that's no secret!"

It is no secret that God thinks you are a wonderful person. In a thousand different ways, God says to you and me, "I love you," as though you were the only one God had to love.

The Bible begins in Genesis with God saying to Adam, "Where are you?" (Gen. 3:9) and ends in Revelation with the Lord saying, "Behold, I stand at the door, and knock" (Rev. 3:20, KJV). And everywhere in between, a love is proclaimed that is so tenacious it will never let us go.

Sometimes people are so hard on themselves they simply can't believe they are so greatly loved by God. They do not realize that the simple acceptance of that love, the appropriation of it deep within one's spirit, is the beginning of a healthy and vital life. They do not take hold of the reality that to say yes to God's love is to unleash within one's spirit the power that brings victory in life.

Andre Auw has written a little story entitled "Out of Order." It's about a mother trying to explain to her little boy why a popcorn machine doesn't work:

"You can't get any popcorn, child, the machine is out of order. See, there is a sign on the machine."

But he didn't understand. After all, he had the desire, and he had the money, and he could see the popcorn in the machine. And yet, somehow, somewhere, something was wrong because he couldn't get the popcorn.

The little boy walked with his mother and he wanted to cry. And, Lord, I too felt like weeping, weeping for people who have become locked in, jammed, broken machines filled with goodness that other people need and want and yet will never come to enjoy because somehow, somewhere, something has gone wrong inside.

God loves even those people for whom "something has gone wrong inside." Each of us is a creature wonderfully made—a creature filled with paradoxes and contradictions. We believe and we doubt, we hope and despair, we love and we hate. In the complexities and pressures of life, we are susceptible to breaks and jams, to something going wrong inside.

But even then, we are lovable because God loves us and sent God's son to die for us. God comes to those like that popcorn machine who are out of order—those who are locked in, jammed, and broken, but filled with goodness that others need and want yet never get to enjoy. God comes to each of us—a bundle of contradictions—and says, "I think you are wonderful: I love you and will love you forever."

Now, I realize there is so much narcissism and sentimentality surrounding the word *love* that its richness is blurred. *Love* is often used in such corrupt and obscene ways that it has become an outrage to good taste and decent feelings. And yet for the people of God, love remains the first and last word. It is basic to a life lived in all its fullness and passion.

I

Since love is so central to the religion of Jesus and Christians, I want us first of all to allow the Bible to have its say on the subject.

In the Old Testament, God is called steadfast love—a love

that never deserts, a love that you can always count on. God is compassionate loving-kindness—always upholding us, never growing weary. God is faithfulness. We read it over and over again in the Old Testament: God's "mercy endureth forever."

It's amazing how we forget that. God keeps his promise a thousand times. God never fails. God is never a dry well. God is never a setting sun. And yet we forget; the next trial makes us doubt God. So, anxieties and fears disturb us deeply, as if our God were a mirage in the desert.

There is a passage in Isaiah that conveys the depth and permanence of God's love: "I will not forget you. Behold, I have graven you on the palms of my hands" (Isa. 49:15–16, RSV). That word *graven* suggests "deeply carved," "inerasably inscribed," "chiseled." Of course, it's figurative language; God doesn't have hands like ours. But it is a profound statement of how permanent and close we are in the divine consideration.

I remember when I was in junior high school—or maybe it was earlier—the day came when I wrote in the palm of my hand the name of the girl I liked. And, since those girls changed frequently—sometimes more frequently than I liked—I would wash one girl's name off and put another's on my palm. But the real mark of love in those days was to put a girl's name on your palm with indelible ink! Even with that, before long the writing would wear off.

But here God says in Isaiah, "I have placed you in my life—engraved you there—and it is forever; your name is inerasable." What power there is in love like that!

The great preacher Gardner Taylor tells of visiting Vernon Jordan, then the National Director of the Urban League, shortly after the assassination attempt on Jordan's life on May 29, 1980. This gallant national leader was in the painful process of recovery from the wounds inflicted by a cowardly sniper. And he told Gardner Taylor something about what had gone through his mind as he lay there in his own blood on a dark road in a strange city.

Jordan said that he saw himself die, and his life passed before him. But one thing kept coming back to him as he lay

there. When he had been a student living away from home, his
mother had written to him every day. Some letters had been
short, some long. Some had borne news from home, while others had said very little of the family. But always at the end of
each letter, after her signature, his mother had written,
"Remember, son, if you trust God, he'll take care of you."

Vernon Jordan said that out there in the darkness, while he
lay in his blood, his mother's words came back to him:
"Remember, son, if you trust God, he'll take care of you."

Later, when his mother came from Atlanta to Fort Wayne
and stood at his bedside, Vernon Jordan reached for her hand
and spoke not as one of America's black leaders, but as his
mother's child. "Mamma," he said, "you told me that if I trust
God, he'll take care of me. Mamma, thank you."

That's the God of the Old Testament—a love that never
deserts us.

In the New Testament, this concept of God is sustained,
although at times the focus is slightly different. Whereas the
Old Testament reveals a God whose glory is outgoing love,
the New Testament intensifies this quality to the point that
love is almost synonymous with outreach. It means God never
hesitates to take the initiative. God is the inexhaustible lover,
always seeking us. God's love is unconditional, and it is tenacious. It is a love that seeks us out no matter where we go.

I see this love in its most unambiguous form in the death of
Jesus. There are many conflicting theories about the meaning
of Jesus' death. In my own theology I have settled on one fact
on which there is an unbroken agreement among major theologians. In the crucifixion, we see more than a great teacher and
prophet done in by the cruelty of humanity. We see in the
dying Jesus the very love of God in action. The cross is saying,
"Love is the true revelation of God's will; love is to guide all
life; love is the only approach to injury, injustice, indignity."

I don't think it is too much to declare that all Jesus said
and all that he did add up to one long effort to interpret the
meaning of love in life.

In Jesus on the cross, we see the heart of God laid bare; we
see the mind of God displayed—and it is a love unlimited.

The first Epistle of John expresses it concisely: "It is by this that we know what love is: That Christ laid down his life for us" (3:16).

I've seen that kind of divine love reflected in some people I have come to know in my church. I think especially of some parents who never gave up on their children, no matter how much anguish and pain their children brought them. These parents kept extending their arms and their hearts, and they opened before me a window into the reality of God.

A nine-year-old girl once said, "I don't know exactly what a family is, but I do know one thing: Your friends can go off and say they don't want to be your friends anymore, but people can't just go off and say they don't want to be your family anymore."

That child is blessed if she has such a family, for lots of parents do give up on their kids. But those parents whose tenacious love has held on to a child through the hardest, bleakest years are the inspiration of my life. They point to a love that is divine, a love that reaches out to those who have hurt us. In them I see the face of Jesus and the shadow of the cross.

All creation was begun with the generosity of the great lover—God. And it is into such a creation that you and I are born to be like God, preoccupied as God is with love. In this kind of world we are meant to love and live vitally and abundantly. In this kind of world, the nonlovers rub against the grain of the universe and get splinters in the soul. They lose life's vitality and often lose their health.

To love is to live. There is no other life. That is the message of the Bible.

II

Eric Fromm, the brilliant psychoanalyst, speaks of the power of love to transform personality. He writes about his own psychological task: "Therapy is essentially an attempt to help patients regain their capacity to love. If this aim is not fulfilled, nothing but surface changes can be accomplished."

The psychological world is saying love is the way to health; it is the way to personal wholeness; it is the way to cast out the debilitating power of fear. But that is exactly what the Bible has been saying all along!

At the root of all our problems is our inability to give and receive love—I believe Jesus was saying that from his cross raised up at the crossroads of a broken and hostile world. As Karl Menninger says, love is the key to all wholeness because it is the intention of the Creator of life: "Love is the medicine for the sickness of our world."

But I think it needs to be stated even more strongly: "Love or perish." These words come from a book written many years ago by a clinical psychologist, Smiley Blanton. He says those are our only options. I believe him. And I wonder if in this twentieth century our greatest need isn't to discover that the kind of love revealed in the Bible and focused in Jesus is still a live option for us?

III

The love that leads to healthy, vital life is a circular kind of thing. "Beloved, if God so loved us, we also ought to love one another" (1 John 4:11, RSV). This concept of divine love is a constant refrain in the New Testament.

"Love your enemies," says Jesus (Luke 6:27). "No way," say you and I. But there is a way. We can love even our enemies because God first loved us. We can love because though we are twisted, failing, disloyal, apathetic, cowardly, cynical, suspicious, lustful, bitter, acrimonious people, Jesus loved us and died for us. And it is out of this kind of love that we can find strength to love another person.

"Make love, not war," read the placards during the Vietnam war protests in the 1960s. Taken in an entirely different context, those words say something about the realities at the center of Christian life. Yet such an affirmation leads only to despair unless we discern the divine initiative, and unless we see that we are sharing a love given to us by neighbors and friends.

We can love, we must love, we do love—because we have received love. God's love is a circular kind of thing.

Any love that I give is received by another and passed on. And it is the love we receive from others that gives us the energy and the motivation to reach out to love others. I can hear a father speaking about his son, in the words of Louis Evely: "I will love him so much, I will bear with him so patiently, I will forgive him so often that the day will come when he will love me as I love him."

Rudolf Bultmann, the German theologian, once said, "Only one who has been loved can love; only one who has been trusted can trust; only one who has been the object of devotion can give."

A basic Christian belief is that discipleship is always responding to God's initiative, God's love and care for us.

The old story of a newspaper reporter watching a Catholic nun clean the gangrenous wound of a Chinese soldier speaks to this. The reporter said, "I wouldn't do that for a million dollars." "Neither would I," replied the nun, as she continued tending her sick patient.

Love is a circular thing—we believe God loves us, so we go on loving others in God's grace.

Jesus brought a life-giving love to people, and it revived and recreated them. Love's power is awesome. Offer it to somebody and see. Give your love away and you will never be empty. Love will always come back. Risk it and see.

Sometimes, people whose lives are jammed and broken and unfulfilled are walking around screaming, "For God's sake, love me. Love me." They go through a million manipulations to get someone to love them.

On the other hand, healthy, vigorous, vital people are those who walk around looking for someone to love. If you see changes in people who are screaming, "Love me, love me," it is because they realize that if they give up screaming and go out and love other people, they will get the love they need in their own lives. It's hard to learn that loving is a circular kind of thing, but when we do, life is transformed.

When we hear the living Spirit of God calling us to exhibit

tough love in this cruel and darkened world, we are tempted
to back away. It isn't easy to love our enemies and those who
hurt us deeply. It isn't easy to love and care about those
who abuse us. It isn't easy to pray for those who have trampled on us. It isn't easy to love the unlovable.

But before we make up our minds not to love a person, not
to offer mercy to a wounded spirit, we would do well to remember what happened on that cross two thousand years
ago. God's love for the world was not conditioned on our
deserving God's mercy, nor our being easy to love. If it were,
then there would be little hope, indeed.

We killed Jesus. Our world is the kind of world that would
still nail Jesus to a cross. We continue to be sinners. Yet
God still loves us and seeks our good.

There is one general rule of love that can't be argued down
or shaken loose. I, as I am, with all my weaknesses and failures and sins, am loved greatly by God. Therefore, I will and
can, by God's help, love my enemies—love all people of the
human family.

It is that kind of limitless love that can save this planet. And
I can only have that kind of love because God first loved me.

IV

Love always goes beyond feeling to doing. Love is not just a
feeling, not just a sentiment, not just an attitude; love is an
action.

Love is the mainspring of a Christian's life—and the Christian imperative is to share that love in the physical and moral
wastelands of modern life.

Love is at the center of healthy life. That is why Jesus
could command us to love: "I give you a new commandment—
love one another" (John 13:35). And once again, love is always seen in behavior, in deeds, in action.

In the nineteenth chapter of Leviticus, Moses tells the people to love their neighbors just as they love themselves. And
how were they to love? Look after the poor and alien. Don't
pervert justice, and never nurse hatred against your brothers

and sisters. Don't seek revenge, and never cherish anger towards others. That, Moses says, is what I mean when I tell you that God commands you to love.

And then there is that haunting phrase in John when Jesus said, "If there is love among you, then all will know that you are my disciples" (John 13:35).

The living challenge—the great test of whether we belong to Jesus—is not in our words but in our lives. Throughout the New Testament, a life of love is shown as the test of our belief.

And this love has practical, specific implications. How can we be the followers of the peasant Galilean whose primary concern was for the poor and the oppressed if we live in an affluence that is insensitive to the enormous pain and anguish of the world?

How can we be followers of the Prince of Peace, one who loved the world and died to redeem it, if we condone the continuation of the nuclear arms race and through our silence allow the deadly race to escalate, if through our apathy we allow our country to become the belligerent bully of the world, if we refuse to eradicate the seedbeds of violence, despair, hunger, and oppression here and among our brothers and sisters around the world?

How can we be followers of him who came to break down the walls of partition and unite all people if we put external value on people according to their politics, their thoughts, their color, their sex?

How can we be followers of one who made limitless love the rule of his life and said to the very end, "I love you even if you destroy me," if we still live in hatred and animosity with any nation on the face of the earth?

We must never forget that Jesus said, "If there is love among you, then all will know you are my disciples."

The power of that love is incalculable. Remember the story of *Beauty and the Beast?* When the beautiful princess kissed the ugly beast, he was transformed.

There is a beast in all of us—in every nation, in every home and church—that part of us we are ashamed of or driven to hide or deny. But Jesus says love is a live option. The beast can be kissed. We can be transformed. Love can change that ugliness into something beautiful.

Your world, your city, your home, your child desperately need to be kissed. God sends you to do just that.

Don't let the enormity of the task of loving overwhelm you. You don't have to solve all the world's problems by sundown. Just begin. Offer love someplace. Kiss the beast and transform an ugly situation. Do it. Put it to work today.

Love takes more than sincere desire and good feelings. (I love the *Peanuts* cartoon showing a dejected Charlie Brown on the pitcher's mound saying, "How can we lose when we are so sincere?") Love takes action! Translate that sincere desire into one act of generosity, one act of love, one kiss of the beast, and a new world will be on its way.

You can't end racism today; you can't end the arms race today; you can't end the loneliness of a friend's old age today; you can't put everyone to work in your city today; you can't wipe away every trace of pain today that years of estrangement have brought to the heart of a friend or family member. You can't solve all those problems that baffle the world today.

But you are capable of one specific act of love and generosity and compassion—one act that will be a link in the movement to create a new and beautiful world of peace and justice and healing.

And God in the divine mystery will take your single deed, your one kiss of the beast, and multiply its significance.

If each one today said, "Yes, love is the answer to hatred and fear," and reached out in kindness to another human being who needs us, we could change the world.

Love always goes beyond feelings, and it always goes beyond those closest to us. Love is to be shared with the world.

One of the great joys of being a pastor is to see so many people giving themselves so generously to the cause of love. Love flows freely and easily in them because they know God's rich love for them. They are the healthiest, the most vigorous, the most beautiful people I know.

In the last act of John van Druten's play, *I Remember*

Mama, there is a scene about such a person—Uncle Chris. Uncle Chris has just died, and the relatives have gathered to read the will. While most of them have considered Uncle Chris a good-for-nothing and an embarrassment to them, they didn't want to miss this event.

Mama comes in to announce that there seems to be no will and no money either. But there is a notebook that is an account of the way he spent his money which she is ready to read to them. "You know how Uncle Chris was lame?" she asks, "how he walked with a limp? It was his one thought, lame people. He would have liked to have been a doctor to help them. Instead he helped in other ways. I'll read you the last page of his notebook, 'Joseph Spinelli. Four years old. Tubercular left leg—$377.18. Walks now. Esta Jensen. Nine years old. Club foot—$217.50. Walks now. Arne Solfeldt. Nine years. Fractured knee cap—$442.16;'" And just then, in the scene, the boy, Arne Solfeldt, comes running into the yard where they could see him. Arne's mother is overcome, for she knew nothing about what Uncle Chris had done. And then, after a moment, Mama continues, "It does not tell the end about Arne. I'd like to write, 'Walks now.'"[1]

To a world that is broken and limping—a world soaked in the blood of war, torn with strife and conflict, ruptured by prejudice and fear, suffering from hunger and disease—God sends you and me to love. It's the greatest gift we can make.

"Walks now!" Let it be.

Part Two

Getting Whole
And Staying That Way

Chapter Four

You Can Be Healed

I am a little reluctant to tell you that you can be healed, that you can make your way to wholeness and stay that way in a vital and passionate life.

The healing field is peppered with too many charlatans and devotees of the lunatic fringe, too many ruthless egotists who prey upon trusting people in their hour of trouble. And so I hesitate to proclaim to you the powers of healing.

Healers are everywhere. While I was on sabbatical in Africa in 1978, I had been asked to do a training project for the Episcopal Church in Liberia. A good number of people came to the workshops and appeared grateful for my efforts. But the real action was down the road. A healer had come to town, and great excitement surrounded her. The city of Monrovia, Liberia, was filled with the news that this woman would heal you of sickness and remove evil spirits.

I was curious, so I followed the crowd to this great woman—and surprise! When I least expected to see one from my own home, there she was—from Pasadena, California. I had lived in Pasadena eleven years at that time and had never heard of her—but in Africa she had a healing hand! And that was powerful to behold.

All Saints Church in Pasadena, where I have the privilege to minister, has been at work for many years on a vast array of projects for the healing of our community and the wider world. To name a few, we are an official place of sanctuary for Central American refugees, have formed an interfaith center to reverse the arms race, carry out a street ministry to provide shelter for the homeless and food for the hungry, and maintain a skills center to help secure entry level jobs for the unemployed. We affirm through our justice ministries that the most important moment of worship is when we step out of the church into the city to bear witness to a new quality of life and a new order of society.

Yet I realize that in our church and the Pasadena community there is a deep need for personal healing. If we commit our energies to work for a more just society without also dealing with the inner brokenness in our own lives, we are impoverished and our effectiveness is diminished.

Several years ago, I decided to have a healing service with the laying on of hands at the main Sunday morning celebration where nearly twelve hundred people had gathered to worship.

I was apprehensive that very few would respond to my call to come forward to the altar for the laying on of hands for healing—that ancient rite of the church. I had shaped the call broadly, so people would understand that all kinds of needs could be brought to the altar: "You with painful physical sickness, come; you with deep discouragement on your mind, come; you with a spirit that is burdened with guilt, come; you with a relationship in the anguish of estrangement, come; you with a hopeful prayer for a sick child, come; you with the burden of a broken world on your heart and its healing in your prayers, come."

Some need very deep in that congregation was touched, for nearly a thousand people came forward in hope of the healing touch of God through the laying on of hands. We had not planned on such a response, so the service took nearly three hours! Yet its power was awesome. And countless people wrote to share with me the profound inner healings, personal transformations, and physical healings they had experienced that Sunday. We now have this type of healing service each year, and the response is always overwhelming.

And yet I must admit that I still have apprehensions in proclaiming that you can be healed. For healing through religion is a strange and complicated arena.

I visited a sick parishioner one day in a Pasadena hospital. After we had talked for a little while, I had a prayer with her. Then I went over to the woman with whom she shared the room—a real Boston dowager—and chatted with her. At the conclusion of my brief chat, I said, "I'd like to have a prayer for your recovery before I leave."

Sitting up a bit more stiffly in her bed, the lady replied, "That will be quite unnecessary, young man. I'm being prayed for in Boston." The tone of her answer made it unmistakably clear that prayers at her bedside in Pasadena were quite pointless, since she possessed a direct line to headquarters.

Healing through religion is a strange and complicated arena.

Have you seen a product on the market called "Trouble Dolls"? It is a large doll with a pouch of small dolls. The instructions read, "In my land of Guatemala the Indians tell this old story. They teach that when you have troubles, share them with your dolls. Remove one doll for each problem. Before you go to sleep, tell the doll your trouble. While you are sleeping, the dolls will try to solve your troubles. Since there are only six dolls, you are only allowed six troubles a day."

Strange things go on in the world of healing. Bizarre claims are made. As a result—and understandably—the possibility of healing through faith has become suspect. And that is why I hesitate to proclaim that you can be healed.

And yet—I proclaim it. For in spite of all that goes on in the name of "faith healing," I still have a tenacious belief in the healing power of God to transform us physically, spiritually, and emotionally.

At the very center of the Christian faith is a bold proclamation that we can be healed, and at the heart of life dwells a power great enough to transform the world. I believe that.

I

I remind you of what you probably already know.

You can never talk about health and speak only of the body, or only of the mind, or only of the spirit.

Each of us is made in one piece—all tied together in a unit. There is not one tissue in our bodies that is removed from the influence of the mind or the spirit.

The theologian Paul Tillich used to talk about "unhealthy health"—because health isn't merely the absence of sickness, but the presence of mental, spiritual, physical well-being. That is what people mean today when they talk about holistic medicine—medicine that recognizes this interconnectedness of mind, body, and spirit.

Norman Cousins, who is now on the faculty of the UCLA School of Medicine, has become a chief proponent of this point of view. In books such as *Anatomy of an Illness* and *Human Options,* he challenges the medical profession with the constant assertion that treatment of disease is incomplete if it is only confined to diagnosis, administration of medicine, and other clinical procedures, and that treatment becomes complete only when the patient's own resources and capacities are fully engaged in the healing process.

Many physicians today are beginning to understand that we must also be treated in the context of our social environment—our relationships with others. Jesus was the forerunner of this concept. He points us toward health when he says, "You shall love the Lord your God with all your heart, and with all your soul, and with all your mind" (Matt. 22:37, RSV). That is the greatest commandment. It comes first. And the second is like it: "You shall love your neighbor as yourself" (v. 39, RSV).

Love God with your total being and love all members of the human family. That brings health. That is wholeness.

John A. Redhead, in *Getting to Know God,* tells a story that brings us into the center of this issue. A man came to a physician with every symptom of serious illness. But when the doctor examined him, he found the man to be organically sound and sent him on home.

In two weeks he was back. "Doctor, I want you to examine me again, for I am at my wit's end. I feel very bad. I am nervous and upset. I can't eat or sleep. I am in great pain. I'm totally miserable."

The physician repeated extensive examinations and tests and again could find no physical cause for illness.

"As far as I can see," he said finally, "there is nothing wrong with you physically. Your body is not functioning normally, to be sure; but I find no evidence of organic trouble."

The doctor went on to confront the man: "What is going on in your life? Do you have something on your conscience? Have you done something wrong? Is your heart burdened with some guilt?"

The patient was insulted and angrily said that he had come for medical advice and not a sermon. Then he turned and stalked out.

Weeks later he returned in a different spirit. "Doctor," he said, "I want to confess that you put your finger on the truth of my illness. I have done something very wrong."

He went on to tell of how he had stolen money from his brother when his brother trusted his business into his keeping while he was living abroad. No one knew about his stealing or could find it out. But, his conscience knew it—and the disease of guilt infected his whole body.

"How much can you pay your brother right now?" asked the doctor.

"Two thousand dollars."

"Then write the check and compose a letter of confession to your brother—including your plan to repay him the rest of what you owe."

They enclosed the check in the letter, sealed the envelope, and walked together to the mailbox. As the man dropped the letter into the mailbox, his face showed he had dropped a great burden from his life.[1]

The man in this story was unquestionably sick. His body was ill. But to give him some chemical prescription or treat him in ways other than spiritually would have been malpractice. Guilt—a spiritual problem—had affected his entire organism to the point that his body stopped functioning well. But when his guilt was lifted, he began the process back to fullness of health.

Each of us is a mind-body-spirit-environment all tied up together. However, I believe we are more spiritual than we are physical. Bruce Larson, in his extraordinarily helpful book, *There's a Lot More to Health Than Not Being Sick,* says "our bodies are barometers of our inner non-tangible experiences, thoughts, fears, resentments, hopes, joys."[2] So physical healing often must be the byproduct of a deeper healing of the mind and spirit.

The healing force is inside us. That is the way God made us. But what we believe with our minds and what is going on in our spirits have a profound effect upon activating or thwarting the healing force.

We move in the direction of our hopes or fears. Every emotion, every thought, every belief makes its registration on the body's system. I would go so far as to say that ninety percent of our illnesses have real spiritual and emotional connections.

So be aware that trust rather than suspicion, hope rather than despair, love rather than hate, grace rather than hostility can activate those powerful healing forces in the body. Good health involves the whole person.

II

There is an incredible healing power in the human body.

In fact, one of the greatest forces in the human body is the natural drive to heal itself. Franz Ingelfinger, the late and much beloved editor of the *New England Journal of Medicine,* once pointed out that what patients need most of all is assurance that their own healing systems are beautifully designed to handle most of their complaints.

I feel very much at home with the remark made some years ago by the great physiologist, Dr. Walter B. Connor, of Harvard Medical School: "When you understand a great deal about the human body and its resources for health, you wonder why anyone is ever sick."

The healing force is inside you and me. That is the way God made us. And today many doctors of the soul, as well as doctors of the mind and body, are saying that what we believe has a profound effect upon activating or thwarting that healing force.

Hope, trust, love—these beliefs and emotions tend to produce a responsive chemistry. We move in the direction of our hopes and fears.

The mind and the soul have unbelievable power over the body. I have seen people die almost instantly when they had lost the will to live—and I've seen people transformed and put on the road to full health when hope took the place of fear. And they recovered because their hope, their confidence that they could get well, actually affected the chemistry of their bodies.

Norman Cousins says that nothing is more wondrous about the fifteen billion neurons in the human brain than their ability to convert thoughts, hopes, ideas, beliefs, and attitudes into chemical substances.

Everything begins, therefore, with belief. What we believe is a powerful determiner of our health and our sickness. Hope, trust, love—these beliefs and attitudes activate that powerful healing force deep within you.

III

Health and sickness remain great mysteries that elude us.

We know of people who were pronounced healthy in their annual checkup by the medical experts and dropped dead within a week. And we also know people who break every rule of good health and yet who are never sick—and look as though they will live forever.

We know we can get sick from unhealthy thoughts and a twisted spirit. But it is also unquestionably true that we can have beautiful thoughts and a graceful spirit and still get grievously ill.

Over the years I have prayed with sick people who had high hopes and authentic love and bold trust, yet who have not gotten well. And I have had experiences with others who are distant to everything spiritual, who have no apparent gratitude for life's goodness, yet who are miraculously healed.

The mysteries of the relationship of mind, body, and spirit will never be fully explained—not by the most brilliant physicians and scientists nor the wisest theologians.

Health is a mystery, and we do a person a gross disservice to indicate she is sick with cancer or any other illness because of her negative thoughts. The foolish, simplistic dimension of that analysis insults the mind. To state that body, mind, and spirit are related is one thing. But to indicate that there is a direct, precise, calculable correlation among the three is quite another—that would be magic, not faith. Religion involves trusting in the midst of life's enigmas—it is full of mystery.

But there is some illumination to this mystery, for at the center of life is the Spirit of the Living Christ, who is powerful to heal. At the heart of the Christian faith is the affirmation that a power is at work in you and me. We can be open to this power, aligned with it, in tune with it—and miracles do happen.

Albert Einstein said we had two choices in life—to live as if all life were a miracle or to live as though nothing were a miracle. I choose to believe in miracles.

IV

According to the Public Health Department at UCLA, a survey has been done which determined that only 6 percent of the American population has optimum health. That leaves most of us out. We are dealing with life on two cylinders, or at least with much less than our maximum capacity.

So many of us are sick of being sick. We are depressed with being depressed. We are enervated by the emptiness of life.

But we can be healed; we can live a vigorous and passionate life with all its wholeness. And for those who seek such a life, I suggest three theological principles that can serve as a guide into the healing light:

(1) *God wants us to be healed.* Jesus touched the broken and bruised, the sad and lonely, the wayward and disloyal, the depressed and anxious ones—touched them and released within them that powerful force of healing.

The God Jesus reveals is a God who wants life to be good, abundant, happy, healthy, peaceful. That is the divine will for each of us.

I find it infuriating to see people harboring false and unworthy ideas about God's will. We attribute to God wars, epidemics, diseases, tragedies. We speak of God's willing the most horrendous disasters. Catastrophes are called "acts of God." In my opinion, there are few more blasphemous phrases in the English language.

I knew a beautiful eighteen-year-old girl, a champion gymnast, who was totally paralyzed in a gymnastic accident. As I visited her in the hospital and tried to minister to her, her mother kept telling her that her paralysis was God's will. I thought of John Wesley's words, "Your God is my devil." A God who willed that lovely girl to be paralyzed? How could we worship or love such a God? There is one thing we must never say in the midst of a tragedy: it is the will of God.

Jesus taught us to pray in the Lord's Prayer, "Thy will be done on earth as it is in heaven." But so many lies are told about that prayer. So much evil has been tolerated under its protection.

Far too many people, when they pray, "Thy will be done," think of lonely grief, wasting sickness, premature death, social disorders. I believe that interpretation misses the primary thrust of Jesus' ministry. For the miracles of Jesus point us to a different view of what God wants for us: healthy bodies, healthy homes, healthy cities.

If we get close to Jesus, who spent an inordinate amount of time delivering people from paralysis, insanity, blindness, we see the will of God in positive terms. God's will means happy homes, estrangement overcome. God's will does not mean slums and urban decay; it means the eradication of those cesspools of despair. God's will does not mean children who are walking skeletons from abysmal hunger; God wants a world of beautiful children. God's will means peace, not war. Remember, the first heart to break in any tragic experience of evil is God's heart.

"Thy will be done." Be careful how you pray those words. It is no moan of resignation. It is the declaration of life and vitality and peace and beauty and transformation.

"Take up your bed and walk." "Once I was blind and now I can see." That's the will of God. We who seek health must fill our minds and hearts with this positive understanding of

God's hopes for us—and these thoughts will release those healing powers deep within us.

(2) *Prayer brings us into union with divine energy.* Imagination is prayer's greatest tool. As you pray, ponder; brood about your life in the presence of God; get a mental picture of the life or the relationship you wish to attain. Imagine yourself walking again tall and straight; imagine yourself released from the bondage of cocaine; imagine yourself in the closest, most intimate, loving, passionate relationship with your spouse; imagine yourself free of cancer. And frame those images with hope. All of this brings you into union with the healing force deep within you.

Prayer issues out of what we believe about God. If we believe God wants us whole and well and grieves with us when we are not, then our prayer is the effort to align ourselves with the recreative healing powers of the divine spirit.

Prayer for healing is not an attempt to change God's mind or to bring God to our way of thinking. True prayer isn't directed at overcoming the divine reluctance, nor is it a campaign to persuade God to do something God otherwise would have left undone.

Prayer is not magic. True prayer lets God be God. And prayer then allows us to be open to receive what God already wants us to have. Prayer is a hand reaching out to receive the amazing, graceful gifts of God. This whole process then allows the great force of God latent within us to work for our health.

God's power dwells in us. We don't create it. We don't impose it. But kneeling in prayer, we open ourselves to receive that reality. And then astonishing things can happen!

Jesus often said that when we are in union with this loving power, there is nothing it cannot do. "Everything is possible to one who has faith" (Mark 9:23). "Everything is possible for God" (Mark 10:27). Jesus set no limit on the power of the spirit. Miraculous events take place when we say yes to God and unite ourselves with the inner healing power that moves us toward our images of health.

(3) *God wants all things to be united and made whole.* The disruption between a father and son, the estrangement of

wife and husband, the barriers between two sisters, the bitterness and jealousy between races, the hostilities between
nations—God wants to heal that sickness.

A person can't be fully whole in a broken world. A doctor
could cure disease in a person, but health and wholeness
would not necessarily be the result if that person's relationships with others were blocked or damaged. A healthy life
recognizes our inextricable ties to our spouses, our employers,
our brothers and sisters of the world.

So much of popular religion today would lead us to believe
all that is required for a healthy, prosperous, virtuous life
is to accept a few simple truths and think positively about
them. Certainly, they say, don't get yourself involved in con-
troversial issues that may burden the heart.

But I would contend that healthy, vigorous, beautiful, passionate life is tied to the health of the world. We cannot be
fully whole in a broken world. We cannot walk fully upright in
a world bent with oppression. We cannot be fully healthy in a
world that cries out in suffering and in pain.

Love your neighbors. Heal the world. Bind up its brokenness. Wipe away its tears. Soothe its wounds. That, says Jesus,
is the way into real health and beauty and joy.

V

Yes, I know that much of this chapter sounds strange to our
secular minds. I ask you not to be so dogmatic as to claim we
know all the processes of nature and the laws that govern this
fragile and intricate creation. Miraculous things can happen—not by suspending laws but by working out laws we
don't yet understand.

There is mystery in all of this. But at the center is the
Christ who wants to heal. We are looking at the edge of this
new frontier of healing. The riddles remain. The dark mysteries perplex. Our healing ultimately depends on how boldly we
are willing to trust God in the midst of life's mysteries.

You know the legend of Atlas in Greek mythology, who is
condemned to uphold the heavens and the earth on his

shoulders. So many of us still live like him, carrying the load of this complex, baffling world on our backs.

A number of years ago I was in St. Patrick's Cathedral on Fifth Avenue in New York City. I stood on the steps of the cathedral and looked across Fifth Avenue to Rockefeller Center to that massive statue of Atlas, bent over with the world on his shoulders. Then I went inside the cathedral and walked up to the altar, over which hung a massive crucifix—a figure of the suffering Jesus on a cross. Standing there at the altar, if I turned around, I could almost see the Atlas across the street.

I have often thought of that experience in St. Patrick's when I struggle with the seeming contradiction between human suffering and divine goodness. For I believe those two symbols—a bent-over Atlas and a welcoming cross—represent our contemporary world.

When the lights of our world go out and suffering comes to us, we can be Atlas—bear the burden of that tragedy on our backs and seek its explanation. Or we can be a disciple of Jesus and hear him say from his cross, his arms outstretched, "Come to me, all of you who are weary and overburdened, and I will give you rest!" (Matt. 11:28, PHILLIPS)

When we are open and united to this God of Power, almost anything is possible.

Chapter Five

God's Power and Your Ambition and Failures

Carl Sandburg once said, "We all want to play Hamlet."
Martin Luther King, Jr., called this desire the "drum major instinct." We all want to be important and achieve some kind of distinction. In some part of us there is that determination to lead the parade.

Alfred Adler, one of the founding spirits of modern psychiatry, calls this drive for power and achievement the dominant impulse in human nature. We are quick to detect this desire for achievement in another person and tend to be provoked by it. But in all fairness, we need to admit that in a thousand subtle ways we, too, have tried to be drum majors and make our way to the front of life's parade. After all, who wants to be last or insignificant?

I remember a period in the 1960s when success was out of fashion. Even in the church, being successful was equated with faithlessness—anyone ministering in a growing, successful church was thought to be compromising the faith, and great achievement was felt to tarnish the armor of God.

I say such talk is theological rubbish! Anyone who wants to fail is sick. Jesus never condemned ambition. Never! He did not degrade our assertiveness.

We all want to be somebody, to succeed, to achieve something glorious. That is healthy. That is the way God made us. The Bible says each of us is a glorious creature—a little less than God. God created us in the divine image, made us to be co-creators of something beautiful and lovely and wonderful, to be achievers and winners in life. God wants us to live in such a way that our lives really matter to the world.

61

Psychologists tell us that we need this sense of importance, that everyone needs some success stories. If we can't find them in the hard world of reality, we tend to seek them in fantasy. As one little girl said, "All my dreams come out the same way. I am always someone important."

Jesus would understand. He saw the world as more than just something to be redeemed. He saw it as something to be enjoyed and delighted in. Jesus came among the people proclaiming a full, joyous, abundant life for all—a life of significance and achievement. God has given us the equipment to become genuinely important. And with all this, God gives us the desire to excel and be someone that counts. Because of that, we sing better operas and preach better sermons, and create more effective corporate organizations. And we become more authentic people.

J. Wallace Hamilton tells of a Methodist Bishop, examining a class of candidates for the ministry, who asked them if they had a strong desire for preeminence in their chosen work. To a person they replied, in humble accents, that such was not their desire. "Men," said the Bishop, "you are a sorry lot—all of you." He went on to say Jesus had fired people's ambition and helped little people to be great. "But just be sure it is real greatness you get."

The drum major instinct, the desire to achieve, the drive to succeed, the aspiration for significance can be misused. It can produce insensitive behavior. It can distort our priorities. It can cause us to elbow people out of the way in our struggle to reach the front of the parade.

Does that mean our desire for achievement must be squelched, repressed? No. But it must be focused in the right direction. Our desire for achievement comes from the Divine Spirit's moving in the deep places within us. God has made us for greatness, and a life that is full and abundant and successful is possible. But this will happen only if we live with the grain of the universe—only if we live as our Creator has destined us.

Jesus took this enormous drive for greatness in us and

redirected it away from ourselves toward the entire human family. He never condemned ambition. He did not degrade our assertiveness; he redirected it.

One day, James and John, the sons of Zebedee, brought all of this into focus in a candid moment with Jesus (Mark 10:35–45). They knew the Master was on his way to the final conflict in Jerusalem. And they came to Jesus and asked to be preeminent among the disciples. They said to him, "Grant us the right to sit in state with you, one at your right and the other at your left, in your glory."

Such bald assertiveness makes us catch our breath. Yet that is the astounding realism of the Bible. On the way to the cross, the disciples were hassling among themselves about who would be greatest.

It was an unseemly squabble as the Savior went to his death, yet it is typical of our human ambitions. James and John wanted to lead the parade; they wanted to be somebody; they wanted to be great. And it is significant that the strong, gentle Christ did not chastise them. Instead, he redirected their attention. He refocused this ambition away from the self as the goal.

"Yes, John and James, you can be important and significant persons. That is all possible if you follow my way into life. You can be great if you are willing to be a servant. You can be first if you are willing to be the slave of all."

That's an incredible encounter with Jesus. He turned on the lights by which his disciples could grope their way into authentic greatness.

To be of value in this world is ultimately not to *have* something, but to *be* something . . . one who serves.

Albert Schweitzer spoke to the graduating class at an English boys' school in 1935. His words are still fresh and relevant: "I do not know what your destiny will be. Some of you will perhaps occupy remarkable positions. Perhaps some of you will become famous by your pen or as artists. But I know one thing: The only ones among you who will be really happy are those who have sought and found how to serve."

I

God made us for greatness. God shaped our souls in such a way that we need success and achievement. However, life's reality is that our paths are littered with heartbreaking defeats and failures.

Vince Lombardi, the late Green Bay Packer coach, once said, "Winning isn't everything. It's the only thing."

But, Coach, some of us have lost. And those instant replays of our disgrace burden our hearts.

We seek a power that can transform these defeats into victory. We cannot make our way to wholeness and stay there unless we can tap into a power that deals with our failures. And that redeeming power lies at the very core of the Christian tradition.

Out of my own experience, I know that from the death and resurrection of Jesus has come the most powerful spiritual force the world has ever known. From this Jesus who rose victorious over the brutality and bleakness of that cross on Calvary's hill has come power to start life all over again, to pick up the pieces and claim our full potential.

There is a powerful, life-giving story in the New Testament about the way Jesus dealt with the failure of others (John 20:19–23). Come with me to the Upper Room where the disciples are hiding after the crucifixion—their total existence filled with doubt and uncertainty. Fear and grief and disgrace are written on every apostle's face. They have failed Jesus. They are cowards. They have humiliated themselves. When Jesus needed them the most, they fled into the night. Now they are ashamed, their self respect wounded and raw.

Then, suddenly and magnificently, Jesus, who is alive, comes and stands in their midst and says, "Peace. . . . Come, my friends. Take my love, my acceptance, my forgiveness. A new life awaits you."

That is the spiritual force of the central belief of the Christian faith: Jesus was the conqueror over death and failure and humiliation. And the disciples could live in that victory and its power.

When we fail, we desperately need a chance to try again. And the resurrection of Jesus—and that scene of Jesus embracing with forgiving love his disgraced disciples—gives us hope that it just might be possible.

Easter is for all who have had a shadow cast across their lives—for those who have gotten kicked in the stomach with bad news, for those whose consciences are heavy with things done that ought not to have been done. The risen Christ comes to us to offer us pardon—a new beginning—and a future full of vibrant hope.

It has taken me nearly a lifetime to begin to understand that winning is not avoiding losing. Rather, it is accepting my losses, acknowledging my failures—and then knowing the power of Christ is at work within me to bring out some kind of victory.

Jesus' resurrection is the central foundation for Christian life. It is a story of the victory of life over death and forgiveness over sin and love over hatred and hope over despair. It is a story that strikes a responsive chord deep in our hearts. Death could not hold Jesus. Hatred could not ultimately destroy him. He lives in the world and in us today. That belief is at the very center of the Christian tradition. It is the answer for both our ambitions and our failures.

II

I am quite aware that this affirmation of the Resurrection belief poses problems for many modern women and men. It is shrouded with mystery for me also.

Several years ago I had spent a few days away working on my sermons for Good Friday and Easter. As I was driving home, I noticed a large marquee outside a motel which read, "Do you have your Easter reservations?" I thought to myself—"Plenty! Plenty!"

But those problems and difficulties don't diminish Easter's integrity in my eyes. In fact, it seems to me, more and more as I grow older, that the resurrection story is blurred by its very brightness! Deeper and more lasting than the one hundred and one questions, asked and unasked, which cluster around this mystery of the resurrection is this one great central truth: Death could not hold Jesus. Hate did not ultimately destroy him. He lives.

And the corresponding reality for our own lives is that death is not the end for us. I trust St. Paul was right: "This corruptible must put on incorruption, and this mortal shall have put on immortality" (1 Cor. 15:53, KJV). God is not the God of unfinished business.

This question of eternal life is central to us. For the life of Franz Schubert, who died at age thirty-one and left a great unfinished symphony, is a parable of all human life. Even if we live threescore and ten years, our lives are still unfinished.

The very character of God is at issue here. In this ecological era, we judge ourselves harshly if we waste and exploit the resources of the earth. But if death ends all, then of all the wasters, God is the worst. Does God produce great people and then throw them away half-finished? Does God create capacities God never uses, possibilities God never fulfills? I don't believe that.

Without the eternal world where the dead are alive with God, a closed door is the ultimate symbol of the universe: A closed door for our lives, a closed door for our families, a closed door at last for all life. The ultimate symbol for this vast, creative, dynamic process of which we are a part—a closed door? I don't believe it.

God is the God of life. God is the God of open doors. This belief can give us courage as we walk inevitably towards death.

An American sailor wrote this letter to his parents during World War II, which, in a simple way, gathers up all the profound dimensions of passionate living in the face of death: Mom and Dad, if you hear that our cruiser has been sunk and that no one has survived, don't grieve for me. The sea in which my body sinks is also the hollow of the hand of my Savior, from whom nothing can separate me!

III

But why are we talking about death here? Because we must first confront our deaths creatively and courageously before we are capable of gaining victory over those failures that litter our earthly pilgrimage.

In his own straightforward way, George Bernard Shaw once pointed out that, for all the medical statistics about a lowered death rate, the ultimate statistic remains the same: One out of one dies.

Life is so fragile and transitory. It can be gone tomorrow and yet most of us avoid that thought—until the reality is thrust unambiguously upon us.

In Herman Wouk's powerful novel, *The Caine Mutiny,* there is a scene in which a newly promoted sailor goes from the engine room to his new battle station on the deck—just as a Kamikaze pilot strikes. The sailor is killed. And Wouk's character Willie Keith lights a cigar given to him by the sailor two days before:

> With the smoke of the dead sailor's cigar wreathing around him, Willie passed to thinking about death and life and luck and God. Philosophers are at home with such thoughts, perhaps, but for other people it is actual torture when these concepts—not the words, the realities—break through the crust of daily occurrences and grip the soul. A half hour of such racking meditation can change the ways of a lifetime. Willie Keith crushing the stub in the ashtray was not the Willie Keith that had lit the cigar. That boy was gone for good.[1]

Death's deep sorrow—or maybe death's insult—is that a human being is lost to the world. This person, loved by the survivors, is lost to those loved ones. This unique *I* who laughs and loves, worries and weeps, who dances and dreams, sings and sins, preaches and prays—this *I* will be lost to the world when I die. And so it is with death for all of us. You cannot be replaced. You are gone.

And yet, the Christian tradition asserts boldly that passionate, full life awaits us if we find the courage to walk toward our death. In the resurrection of Christ, death is conquered. We mortals are now free. We can live without fear. Death has no more dominion over us.

Don't misunderstand me. I'm not enthusiastic about death! I doubt I shall ever want to die—not so much because I fear death, but because I love life. I love my life with the people whom I cherish and with whom I have a history. The tension in me isn't between life and death, but between this life and the next.

My father used to caution me when driving with me in my beginning years behind the wheel of a car, "Son, be careful. Heaven is my home, but I'm not homesick." I'd say that is a healthy, robust, Christian attitude in the face of death—even Jesus pulled back at first!

No, I face death not with enthusiasm but with readiness; not with surrender but with willingness to go if I must; not with fear but with trembling at the adventure that awaits me. And I believe that if I can look at my death honestly and courageously, I will have released into my own spirit a powerful, passionate energy for living—an energy that will help me fulfill my need to be somebody and help me overcome my failures.

Rabbi Harold Kushner, in *When All You've Ever Wanted Isn't Enough,* recounts a scene from a play on television he had seen many years before but had never forgotten: A young man and a young woman are standing at the railing of an ocean liner. They have just gotten married, and this cruise is their honeymoon. They are talking about how fulfilling their love and marriage have been for them, even beyond their expectations. The young man says, "If I were to die tomorrow, I would feel that my life had been full because I have known your love." His bride says, "Yes, I feel the same way." They kiss and move away from the railing and now the audience can see the name of the ship on a life preserver: TITANIC.[2]

Life's fragility never allows us to forget that we have but a moment to love. That gives a dimension of the greatest ecstasy, passion, and intensity to our experiences of love.

An important part of the ritual of a Jewish wedding is the breaking of the glass by the groom at the end of the ceremony. In the midst of that beautiful, lovely, tender moment of marriage, there is the symbolic intrusion of death. The broken glass at a wedding symbolizes the fragility and transitory nature of life. It says to the bride and groom, "You have but a moment to love. Don't misuse it. Treasure it."

In a similar vein, Abraham Maslow, the famous psychologist, wrote after his heart attack:

The confrontation with death—and the reprieve from it—makes everything look so precious, so beautiful—that I feel more strongly than ever the impulse to love life, to embrace it, and to let myself be overwhelmed by it. . . .

Death and its ever-present possibility makes love, passionate love, more possible. I wonder if we could love passionately, if ecstasy would be possible at all, if we knew we'd never die.[3]

Life is so fragile and transitory. It can be gone tomorrow. To know this reality in those deep places of the heart is to make passionate—and successful—living possible.

IV

"My life is such a failure," she kept saying over and over to me.

"Why do you say that?" I responded, "You show none of the marks of failure."

"My life is boring and tedious. That's my failure."

And it's the failure of many of us. Few would be so bold as to call our affluent, hedonistic, gadget-filled society drab. But so many of us seem dulled to the wonder and glory that is right before our eyes.

Bernard Levin, in an article in *New York Times Magazine* entitled, "In Praise of Enthusiasm," says this:

Wherever you look, jaded palates seek sharper flavors. Leave aside the moral and legal questions raised when fashionable folk in fashionable Park Avenue duplexes sniff cocaine. Does nobody see how very odd such behavior is? And the oddness lies in the fact that such people must have anesthetized themselves against enthusiasm so heavily that only the spurious thrill of poison can break through to their feelings.[4]

In the most affluent society on earth, there is still so much boredom and emptiness. In the midst of plenty, there is a famine of meaning and deep relationships.

I feel this emptiness all around me. There is an aching thirst in our country for meaning, rich fulfillment, passionate living—a thirst for life in the midst of deadness. In a success-oriented society, this is the success we truly crave.

But here, again, the resurrection is God's life-giving solution for our failure to live passionately and vitally. "Why seek the living among the dead?" the messenger asked at the tomb that first Easter. "He is not here. He is risen" (Matt. 28:6). The story of the resurrection is the greatest news to ever break across the earth. That story has an excitement and a joy that reaches the deepest places inside of us. Living in the glory of that event, we can advocate passionate living and play down chic cynicism and cool despair.

We are bound for glory. We are made for something better, and we know it and long for it and search for meaning in life. We know the real joy and glory of life is to be committed to something greater than ourselves and to be rooted in a God who knows us through and through and loves us still—not because we are good or successful, but because we *are*. And this God who loves us raised Jesus from the dead. This God rules creation. This God will have the last word. So we can rejoice in God's glory no matter who or what's on top. And we rejoice not only in God's glory, but in God's power. The resurrection of Jesus released power for us to live life in all its fullness and passion now.

Yes, eternity is opened to us. God will give to those who love God a new life in eternity. That is an essential part of my beliefs. Yet, I long for some sense of resurrection in the midst of this life. Can hate be melted? Can love conquer? Can boredom be overcome? Can failure be redeemed? Is resurrection possible now from hopelessness and confusion and anesthetized feelings?

The resurrection of Jesus is God's resounding and unalterable *yes*. Jesus' life was magnificent. His death was awe-inspiring. Standing beneath the cross, we wonder if the values we see in this man belong to the essence of our life. Looking at Jesus, we ask, "Is that the way successful life is—loving, giving, serving, forgiving, trusting?" The resurrection is God's triumphant *yes*. Such a life is not in vain.

The resurrection validates the life of Jesus; it seals those glorious thirty-three years with God's approval. In the mystery of the empty tomb, God vindicates all Jesus was and said and did. Jesus was the kind of human being God created us to be. The life, death, and resurrection of Jesus proclaim that gentle love is the most powerful force in the world, stronger than hatred and brutality; that peace and justice are realities which beat at the heart of the universe; and that God's care embraces every creature on the face of the globe—none are excluded.

If this affirmation is to have power in your life, you must see it with your own eyes and claim it for yourself. As the Danish theologian, Sören Kierkegaard, once said, "I do not know the truth except when it becomes part of me."

When I hear and see people saying we must break out of the death grip of meeting injury with bitterness, saying we must never be taught to hate another nation again; when I see people saying we can banish suspicion among nations and renounce war and its insanity forever; when I see a person taking the hurts of life, absorbing the agony within herself and forgiving rather than retaliating—I say to myself, you are right. For the death and resurrection of Jesus say those things belong to the stuff of eternity.

In the words of the Fuller Seminary Professor, Lewis Smedes, "When you forgive someone who hurt you, you are dancing to the rhythm of the divine heartbeat. When you forgive you are in tune with the music of the universe. You are riding the crest of love, the energy of the cosmos."[5] That is the power we discover in the resurrection of Jesus. Whenever you discover the power of the Risen Christ that allows you to begin anew in a relationship with someone who has caused you pain, you walk in stride with the living God.

I know this truth because it has become part of me. Over more than thirty years of the ordained ministry I have seen this resurrection power at work, giving life to people too many times ever for me to doubt its authenticity.

I can see some of these people so vividly in my mind's eye:

A man is terminated from his job after twenty-five years of faithful work. But he won't give up; he goes on gallantly trying to end his career with dignity. That's the resurrection power.

A woman is told she has cancer, that her future is bleak and the prospects for healing slim. But she, too, refuses to give up. She continues to live with her devoted husband and children in the confidence that God is good and loving. That's the resurrection power.

A couple experiences the horror of their young child's death. They are scarred, and they know they will limp through life. But they tell me that underneath all the pain and anguish they have found a love stronger than death. And now they are working to help suffering children in Central America. That is the resurrection power.

A husband and wife have found their marriage drying up and all its richness and fun gone. They are unwilling to give up but continue to suffer and love and work on their marriage until a new and beautiful relationship emerges. That's the resurrection power.

A woman cherishes the earth and believes all people are precious to God. She sees in the nuclear arms race a threat to the planet Earth and its people. So she goes to work for peace, even though everywhere she encounters cynicism and apathy. There is little progress and the prospect for arms control and weapon reductions grows slim. Still, this woman does not give up. She believes in tomorrow and she is determined to give it to her children freed of the terror of nuclear war. That's the resurrection power.

These are people who are not bored. Life is not tedious for them. They have no need of drugs to stimulate a jaded palate. These are people immersed in a life that is alive—filled with importance and immediacy. They are bound for glory.

When I see these people before my eyes, I say to myself, "No dead Christ could do that to anyone." He is risen. The spirit of Jesus is let loose in the world, and that power gives us the energy for great and passionate and successful living.

V

In the art of living we seldom achieve success all by ourselves. The struggles are too fierce and the failures too frequent for us to walk alone. We won't journey in wholeness for long if we must do it by ourselves. If we are to overcome failures, courageously face life's fragility, and live life fully and passionately and successfully, we need a cheering section. I've always believed that is important, but in these older years of my life I have come to realize I cannot achieve anything without it.

We all have voices that speak to us from those deep places within, from the emotional cellars of our lives—remembered voices that discourage us and hold us back. I can hear one of those voices now: "George, you're not going to make it. No way. Every time you get determined to make it out of that destructive habit, you screw it up again. You can't do it."

Those voices from our emotional cellars can be destructive, and we can spend a lifetime trying to free ourselves from their tyranny. Some are from the past, some from the present—but all are at work to bring havoc to our lives.

The late Carlyle Marney, a brilliant theologian and loving pastor, talked about untamed terrors in his own emotional cellars. But he said he also had something extraordinary to help him on his way—"balcony people." Marney envisioned in his clear, conscious mind a balcony with a rim around it and filled with people. And those people were standing up and leaning over the railing to urge him on in his endeavors, to cheer him on his way.

We all have a balcony like that filled with people. Some are dead and some still walk the earth with us, but each in his or her own way encourages us and assures us we can succeed. We need to listen to them, linger in their presence, and from them gain hope and courage for the race.

Who is in your balcony? The people who encourage you in life, the people who cheer you on into greatness in the name of God, the people who inspire you to live at your best even in a world at its worst? Make your list. Balcony people are our mentors, our heroes and heroines, our supporters, our friends, our lovers, our positive critics, our leaders.

Let me tell you about my balcony.

I would find my father there. A Greek immigrant, he came to America by himself at age thirteen and worked hard to create a successful restaurant to hand on to his children. My dad never understood why I wanted to go into the ministry. But he always had such life-giving confidence in me. He believed in me. And no matter what I did, my father's confidence in me, in my possibilities, never wavered. He's been dead now almost thirty-five years; still I can almost feel his strong hand on my arm and hear his voice: "Move on, George, onward. There's no time to waste on discouragement. Move on, create a better world, son." Dad's in my balcony.

And there are others, living and dead, whom I've loved greatly and been close to over the years. There is John A. T. Robinson, my theological mentor, who died of cancer at age sixty-five. As I look in my balcony and see John there, the memories are still vivid of our last visit together, when I asked him what he truly believed as he faced his death. This man, whom many credit with precipitating the "Theological Revolution," answered me with these quiet words:

"My faith has served me well, George. Tell that to my critics. The living Christ whom I tried to find in the midst of life, and who lives in me now, will be with me at death. Nothing can destroy that—not death itself. So I trust God, in whom I will live forever."

Yes, John Robinson is in my balcony. And so are many others—a man I knew so well who understood that courage was more than a gun in his hands, a nurse who worked for twenty years on a cancer ward and never ceased believing in God's goodness, a special person who knows me through and through and loves me still.

And then there are a few people who still know how to love in a world poisoned with hatred, who still know how to trust in a world estranged by suspicion, who still know how to be truthful and pure in heart in a world of obscenity and duplicity. They're in my balcony, too.

When I grow weary and the race is hard, I rejoice in the fellowship of "so great a cloud of witnesses" (Heb. 12:1, RSV). When I grow discouraged, it's as though they lean over the balcony and call to me, "Onward, George, onward in the race that God has prepared for you."

It is very important that we realize that those balcony people are ordinary people, flawed people. The reason that grace comes to us so powerfully through the communion of saints is because none of those saints is perfect. But those heroes and heroines have a righteousness in the midst of the flawedness of their lives. That is why they are so important in the balcony of our lives.

We all need our balconies—and our balcony people. For there we find people who can help us overcome self-indulgence and give us encouragement when relationships falter and hope fades and our dreams die in the dark. It is that communion and death-defying unity with those balcony people, dead and alive, that give us courage to keep in the race, to strive for achievement and overcome failures. I think they are singing to us this verse from that great hymn, "For All the Saints":

> And when the strife is fierce, the warfare long,
> Steals on the ear the distant triumph song,
> And hearts are brave again, and arms are strong,
> Alleluia, alleluia![6]

Chapter Six

Created for Community

"You will never know how lonely I am," a young woman remarked poignantly to me in a conversation I was having with a small group of people. Immediately the others nodded in agreement, and one of them said, "I guess that goes for all of us."

Everything in our society seems to validate the fact that loneliness is stamped on America's face and etched deeply into her heart.

Futurist Alvin Toffler says in his powerful book, *The Third Wave,* that from Leningrad to Los Angeles, all kinds of people complain of loneliness and isolation. He writes, "The hurt of being alone is, of course, hardly new. But loneliness is now so widespread it has become, paradoxically, a shared experience."[1]

There is something very deep, something very basic, in us that pushes us toward community. We are so made that we must belong to someone; we must have companions on the journey; we must be attached if we are to live life fully and passionately. It is almost impossible for us to become whole persons and stay that way if we are all by ourselves.

Maybe that's why the most drastic punishment society has yet devised is solitary confinement—isolation from all other human beings. A person in solitary confinement finds that even his heartbeat, ordinarily unnoticed, begins to sound like timpani pounding in his ears.

We all have those painful memories of times when we have felt detached and lonely. Remember those times as a child when you felt no one in the whole world understood you? Remember those moments in adult life when you felt detached from everyone and everything?

Once during my graduate work at Cambridge University, I became grievously ill and spent a number of weeks in an English hospital—away from my family, friends, and colleagues. My academic future was uncertain, my health was in serious question, my career was being seriously tested. But what I remember most clearly about that agonizing experience some thirty years ago was how utterly lonely I felt.

We've all experienced it. With the loss of a job, the loss of a spouse, the loss of a hope, some layer of comfort is ripped away and there we are, having to go it alone. Sometimes our aloneness is symbolized forcefully by an empty chair, an empty bed, an empty office, an empty and aching heart. It all weighs us down, and in those very private cellars of life we feel completely alone.

Robert Raines, in his book, *To Kiss the Joy,* describes such an experience, and I find myself nodding yes:

> Sometimes we experience our aloneness as an annoying, free-floating itch with no place to scratch, a yearning deep within us that will not let us rest, a restlessness to know and to be known wholly, to touch our own deeps and the deeps of another, a restlessness to reach out and feel the heartbeat of creation.[2]

I

We can only live fully in relationship.

God made us that way; it is not our idea. God put deep within us the desire to belong to other people. We are created for community with other human beings.

Now, this need for relationship can manifest itself in strange ways. The story goes that a man returned to his room at the Pasadena Hilton Hotel after a day of hard, challenging business conferences. On the table in his room was the ever-present Gideon Bible. He opened it. In the front were some suggestions on how the Bible could meet our personal needs. One said, "If you are lonely, read Psalm 23." Someone had written beside it in pencil, "and if you are still lonely, call 796-1172!"

There is something very basic in us that pushes us toward community. The noted psychotherapist Carl Rogers describes in a beautiful way this hunger for people and dialogue:

> One thing I have come to look upon as almost universal is that when a person has been deeply heard, there is a moistness in his eyes. . . . It's as though he were saying, "Thank God, somebody heard me. Somebody knows what it's like to be me." In such moments, I have had the fantasy of a prisoner in a dungeon, tapping out day after day a morse code message, "Does anybody hear me? Is anybody there . . . ?" Finally one day he hears some faint tapping which spells out "yes." And he is released from loneliness and has become a human being again.

No one is exempt from this need to belong, to have companionship, to be in community. There is no real life without it.

Biologically, we know that if a child is not cared for by someone, he will scarcely live out the first day. Psychologically, we know that a child withdraws from life and withers away if she does not receive a caring love. Studies have shown that children fail to thrive physically and may even die if they are deprived of touch and companionship! It is scientifically verifiable that life itself depends on relatedness, attachment, belonging.

If this is true in infancy, it never changes as we grow older. A social worker once went to great lengths to secure a way to have an elderly widow from a dark tenement slum spend two weeks in the country. But after only two days of fresh air, warm sunshine, green grass, and shady trees, the woman came home. When the social worker asked her why she had left so soon and so abruptly after so much effort to give her this opportunity, she replied, "Trees ain't people!"

She had discovered the truth that no matter how dark and dirty the streets, her roots and her life were in that slum— there she belonged to her neighbors.

A few years ago, Professor Philip Zimbardo of the University of Southern California wrote, "I know of no more potent killer than isolation. There is no more destructive influence

on physical and mental health than the isolation of you from
me and us from them."

And Dr. James Lynch, the Johns Hopkins University re-
searcher who wrote *The Broken Heart,* says that the new word
from the medical community is that loneliness is the number-
one killer in America. And he has ten years of charts to back
him up on this.

In *The Immense Journey,* Loren Eiseley movingly describes a moment when a human being first walked across
this earth and realized that good and evil would walk with
him forever. It was a new world of terror and loneliness. Then
these words: "For the first time in four billion years, a living
creature had contemplated himself and heard, with a sudden
unaccountable loneliness, the whisper of the wind in the night
reeds. Perhaps he knew, there in the grass by the chill waters,
that he had before him an *immense journey.* "[3]

In this vast universe, knowing how fragile we are, we desperately need comrades to share the immense journey. And
perhaps the highest expression of civilization is not its art
but the supreme tenderness that people are strong enough to
feel and care for each other.

II

Seek diligently for a place where you can belong and be
attached to people who care.

Maybe you need to be given permission to allow someone to
care for you. It is okay to be comforted in your loneliness and
receive the love of a friend and the embrace of a neighbor
and the hand of a companion. It is okay to need to be held.
Yes, I know we should be strong. But I also know we become
deeper, warmer, more understanding of people when we understand and acknowledge our own need to receive love as
well as give it.

If the need to belong to someone is as deep as I believe it is,
churches need to seek more creative ways for this experience
to take place. Dr. Howard Clinebell, the pastoral psychologist
at the School of Theology in Claremont, California, writes

forcefully that an institution is viable to the degree that it
provides opportunities for human growth and fulfillment. I
believe he is right. Churches ought to be places where human
beings grow less lonely.

Now, I am quick to accept the fact that real belonging can't
be programmed—in a church or anywhere else. Keith Miller
tells in *The Becomers* how so many Sunday afternoons while
he was growing up his father would announce to the family
through gritted teeth, "We are going to do something as a
family today—just to have fun together—does everyone understand that?" That hits a raw nerve!

No, I'm quite confident that a community, an extended
family, can't be artificially manufactured by the church. But
a church can provide the setting with trained leaders and
pray that God's spirit will come and give it life and integrity.
And I believe there are few tasks more important in the basic
mission of a church.

The Gospel of John's account of the Last Supper speaks of
this with such power. Jesus' own pain and suffering were
unobtrusively in the background as he talked to the disciples.
At the moment when his world was falling apart with hate
and bitterness, he was thinking of the one thing that could
hold the world together. There in the Upper Room, he broke
the bread of the Eucharist and said to those disciples, "This
is my commandment: love one another, as I have loved you"
(John 15:12).

A real church allows this to happen at the center of its life;
it becomes a setting where people can get together and say to
each other, "I am willing to belong to you, to be a companion
with you; I am willing to share my doubts and my hopes, my
joys and my pains; I am willing to care about your well-being
and your nurture. And in all of this I trust that I can grow in
my love for God and for the world God so greatly loves."

When that kind of care and love come alive in a place, when
the sorrow of one becomes the pain of all and the laughter of
one is the joy of all, then you have a real church. And how
glorious it is. For when we belong to a community of human

kindness and caring love, we catch a glimpse of that divine friendship whose love will never forsake us nor ever let us go.

III

We can live life fully only if we belong to God.

I desperately need to share my life with others, to belong to a group of people who know me best and love me still, to be part of a community that bears my burdens and rejoices in my victories. I want to belong to someone I value.

But the issue of loneliness is much deeper than that. It is a spiritual problem. So it can't be totally remedied by producing another person or another million persons. In fact, we can be lonely even when we are not alone. I remember a New Year's Eve many years ago when I felt that Times Square in New York City was the loneliest spot on the earth!

Persistently we seek solutions for our deep loneliness in the wrong places. Somewhere within our lonely and dissatisfied souls a voice whispers from time to time, "Get a new friend, a new spouse, a new city, a new job—maybe then you'll find what you're searching for."

How foolish we are. No friend or lover, no husband or wife, no community or job will be able to put to rest our deepest cravings for unity or wholeness.

Yes, we do need to belong, and friends and family are vitally important, but it is false and unfair to expect another human being to remedy our loneliness completely. I often wonder if much of the recrimination and accusation and jealousy and repressed anger that go on in marriage are not the result of this false claim that the other person must take our loneliness away.

And if another person can't fix the deep restlessness in the spirit, then we try other remedies. And how those escapes from the loneliness of the spirit line the landscapes of our lives: drugs, overeating, overworking, overdrinking, uppers and downers—and some promiscuous sex as well. All of this to try to anesthetize ourselves against feeling lonely. But we know the relief is temporary at best, and usually the escapes themselves bring even greater pain and anguish.

Today's loneliness has helped to create a lucrative "lonely hearts" industry that purports to help the lonely locate and lasso Mr. or Mrs. Right.

Now, I personally see nothing wrong with admitting one is lonely and using whatever legitimate aids one can find to locate the right companion. But the answer to the deep pain of inner loneliness is not necessarily to be found through the company of another person—however that person is discovered.

Many years ago I was counseling a very lonely woman whose husband had died some years before. One day she very hesitantly told me she wanted to go to one of those agencies that use a computer to match you up with the right person.

"I've been told about a very experienced and expensive one," she said, "and it just might get me the right man."

"Wonderful," I said, "go for it!"

She was very timid about the whole venture, but indeed she did make her application and pay her money. Some months later she called me on the phone. She was nervous and apprehensive; her "computer date" had just called. She said it had been a very strange conversation, and she didn't feel very good about it.

I responded, "But you've spent a lot of money and waited a long time. Why not see what he is like?"

"Only if you are here when he arrives," she responded.

"You've got a deal. I'll be there."

"And wear your clerical collar!" she insisted.

As we waited for the man to arrive, she said, "I just didn't like the insinuations he made on the phone. I'd love it if he were really nice. But I'm not going out with him if he's a disaster."

Well, he was a disaster. Every aspect of him set off negative responses in her and in me. So after a brief conversation with my friend, I explained to him that it was all a mistake and she had decided against going out. He protested strongly, then left in a huff.

In the aftermath, my friend and I sat down and laughed together about the whole experience. Then, very thoughtfully, she said something I don't think I'll ever forget. She said, *"There are some things worse than loneliness."*

Happily, this woman found the inner resources to convert her feelings of loneliness into solitude, and to allow God into the emptiness of her heart. Those inner resources of God's grace watered her desert place and she gradually found life rewarding and full again. She has a terrific husband now. I wonder if she has ever told him about "our" computer date!

We must belong to others. But the ultimate remedy for our loneliness lies deep within us; it is rooted in an eternal God who knows us best and loves us still, a God who can quench the deepest longings of our heart, a God who will never let us down.

Listen to the promise of Jesus to his disciples: "I will not leave you comfortless: I will come to you" (John 14:18, KJV). That's more than just a spiritual uplift in a time of trouble. *Comfortless*—from the Greek word meaning "orphan"— implies abandonment, isolation, desolation, utter loneliness.

"I will not leave you comfortless." Jesus didn't have in mind giving us the external comforts of society. Jesus was speaking about the last loneliness of the soul cut off from both humanity and God. He was promising he would not leave us forsaken by the source of life itself—God.

"I will not leave you comfortless . . . alone, orphaned, abandoned, bereft . . . I will come to you!"

That is the Presence that ends all loneliness, the belonging that will alone meet the deepest needs of our lives. Paul says, "All deserted me. . . . But the Lord stood by me and gave me strength" (2 Tim. 4:16, 17, RSV). That, ultimately, is the answer to our loneliness.

Something very deep in me responds to Maya Angelou who, in *I Know Why the Caged Bird Sings*, describes her lonely childhood as a black girl in the deep South. Recalling how she was shunted back and forth among her several family units— parents, stepparents, grandparents, and friends—she comments, "Of all the needs (there are none imaginary) a lonely child has, the one that must be satisfied, if there is going to be hope and a hope of wholeness, is the unshaking need of an unshakable God."[4]

That's our deepest need. We want to belong to God. We have been created to commune with the Creator. And "Though the earth be moved and though mountains be toppled into the depths, the sea," as the psalmist says (Ps. 46), we want to belong to an unshakable God.

I want to make a confession. Although I have grown up saying and singing the Gloria Patri ("Glory be to the Father, and to the Son, and to the Holy Ghost . . . "), I've never liked it. I've sung it and said it thousands of times, but that "Glory be to the Father" business just never meant much to me—especially the way it is done in most Protestant churches at the oddest moments.

But Ernest Campbell turned me around in a sermon I heard him preach. I had been grumbling inside as we sang that weary piece of music—"Glory be to the Father . . ." But then he shouted, "Listen to the words, really listen: 'Glory be to the Father . . . as it was in the beginning, is now, and will be forever.' That's marvelous. That's what you need."

I've thought frequently about that moment of preaching. For the affirmation of the Gloria Patri *is* what I need—a solid base, an unmovable anchor in this turbulent world. Can you think of anything or anyone else in the world of which those words could be descriptive: "As it was in the beginning, is now, and will be forever"? Only the glory of God.

You can't say it of Exxon or IBM.

You can't say it of stocks and bonds.

You can't say it of Harvard or UCLA.

You can't say it of the New York Mets or the Los Angeles Dodgers.

You can't say it of Hollywood or Broadway.

You can't say it of TV's "Dallas" or "Dynasty."

You can't say it of the Soviet Union or the United States.

You can't say it of your grandmother or your grandson.

The only thing that was in the beginning, is now, and will

be forever is the glory of God. When I allow myself to live in that glory, my life is transformed.

IV

We can participate in God's glory and live life fully only as we become involved in building a compassionate world that prizes human community.

For it is a fundamental truth that we cannot have anything we want most unless we share it. If we want a unity and a wholeness in our own spirits, then we must work at taking down those dividing walls between us and our sisters and brothers of the world.

Compassion builds human community, for it celebrates our solidarity; it affirms that we are created together in one human family to share life. For as an old proverb says, "A sorrow shared is a sorrow halved; a joy shared is a joy doubled." There is no answer to loneliness if we are uninvolved, unconcerned, unrelated to all who seek life and wholeness and rich meaning.

Too often, I'm afraid, the theology of self-fulfillment and the old appeals to spiritual revival and piety have dulled our awareness of the need to eliminate social evil. But the Bible makes it very clear that the ultimate purpose for individual fulfillment, personal renewal, and personal faith is the transformation of the whole world!

All of us want to make our way into a vigorous, healthy, passionate life, and God wants to bless our search. But we must never forget that literally millions have had their dreams of a full life mangled by racism, war, poverty, disease, injustice, and political tyranny. And the Bible's call is clear: to minister to "the least of these" in the community of the world.

Authentic personal growth as a Christian disciple will inevitably energize us in a struggle to see the world changed and peace with justice established.

Some years ago the papers were full of a story about the

death of seventy-eight people in New Delhi, India. There had been a bus accident and in the flaming bus were two castes of Indians. A man tied a rope to a tree, and all eleven "untouchables" climbed out to safety. But seventy-eight died because they would not use the same rope!

We find life in its fullness and wonder and beauty as we are attached to the one human family, or we don't find it at all.

Part Three

Living Passionately From the Inside Out

Chapter Seven

Goodness: It's Commitment, Not Perfection, That Counts

As I look across the landscape of contemporary America, I see that the concept of goodness is not in fashion.

In their freedom to express the realities of American life— a freedom I uphold and defend—some artists point to aspects of life I don't want to look at or listen to. There is in this life coarseness and brutality and distorted sexuality; I know that. But it seems these days we are constantly bombarded with the "underside of life."

Violence seems an accepted way of life. Sex as a value-free, neutral lifestyle often seems to be the emerging, predominant attitude. So much in contemporary society debases moral values and purity; so much is brutal and assaults a gentle spirit; so much is vulgar and corrupts the soul and the mind.

So when I come across this verse in Acts: "They sent Barnabas to Antioch. . . . for he was a good man, full of the Holy Spirit and of faith" (11:24), I wonder if the term *goodness* has any meaning for contemporary Americans, or if they are beyond an appreciation of Barnabas.

He was a good man! Not brilliant or clever or witty or popular, but good. The disciples sent Barnabas to Antioch, where the followers of Jesus were first called Christians. The mother church in Jerusalem believed he was the right disciple to send on that enormously important mission to the Gentile world. He was the kind of person who could take hold of a small, almost amorphous group of people and weld them into a strong Christian community that was to become the first shining outpost for Jesus in the pagan world.

New Testament scholar F. J. Foakes Jackson has written

these arresting words about Barnabas and his traveling companion, Paul:

> Barnabas . . . is one of the most attractive characters in the New Testament. Probably inferior in ability to Paul, he was his superior in Christian graces. He seems to have been utterly without jealousy, eager to excuse the faults of others, quick to recognize merit. . . . Paul's elevation of character makes him scarcely human, while the virtues of Barnabas make him singularly lovable. The Paul of history contributes to the progress of the world, Barnabas and those like him make it endurable to live in.[1]

But if we are honest, is that the picture we get when we read that Barnabas was a "good man"? Or do we see a bland, plodding figure—perhaps even a stuffy, humorless one? If so, perhaps it is because the word *goodness* has fallen on hard times and its meaning has been distorted.

It is not unusual for words to change their connotations over the years. When St. Paul's Cathedral in London was finished in 1716, the king called it "amusing," "awful," and "artificial." And the architect, Christopher Wren, was overjoyed at the royal compliment. For in those days *amusing* meant amazing, *awful* meant awe-inspiring, and *artificial* meant artistic.

Words do change their meaning. And *goodness* has taken on unfortunate connotations today. But we can't live passionately and authentically without it. So I want us to look carefully at goodness—updated and redefined.

I

Goodness in its truest expressions is a beautiful quality.

In a world so soiled with vulgarities—so morally ambiguous, so insensitive to the preciousness of human life, so blatantly dishonest, so callous before the anguish of human need, so dependent on the crutches of drugs—in such a world, a good person is a magnificent offering.

"She is a good woman." Somehow we must rediscover the wonder of that statement. Today we tend to take it as something to say about her if there is nothing else to say.

"He is a good man." Most of us would rather be known as brilliant, clever, witty, brave, popular, or attractive.

Part of the problem is that goodness has come to be associated with that die-hard caricature of Christianity as a wet-blanket religion which represses all normal impulses and smothers every spark of earthy, sensuous joy.

It is tragic that for many of us the concept of goodness is so often unattractive. He might be a good man, but we don't want to go fishing with him. Cold correctness, dull piety, tight-lipped respectability—those are the traits we tend to associate with goodness. I often want to shout, "God save us from people with such 'good traits'!"

As Ronald Goetz writes, we've seen "Christian values twisted in upon themselves which renders truth into smugness, purity into prudishness, justice into status quo, and honor into pride."

Once there was a little girl who encountered an austere, righteous aunt, and the little girl prayed that night, "Dear God, make all bad people good and all good people nice." I have a warm place in my heart for that little girl. She had encountered firsthand one of the reasons *good* doesn't sound good to us anymore.

In fact, an overreaction against so-called "goodness" has taken us to the opposite extreme. Hollywood knows it can be fatal for a movie star to get the image of being a "good" person. They also know that a "G" rating can be the kiss of death for a film. We have reached the point that there almost has to be some foul language, nudity, or bloody violence in the film if it is to be successful, even if they are in no way congruent with the story.

We have become so afraid of strait-laced, judgmental, boring "goodness" that morally objectionable behavior has begun to look good! But even if puritanism is a problem, impuritanism won't save us. The world is in desperate need of good women and good men. But goodness must be redefined—and updated.

I know some good people. But they are unpretentious, spontaneous, fun-loving, attractive, warmhearted, broadminded, and generous. They are positive rather than negative, active rather than passive, and free from fussiness and sanctimoniousness. These people are those who belong to a goodness redefined.

The people I am talking about are not all living in monasteries or convents, but in the midst of secular life, and they live life at its highest level in a world at its worst. Dag Hammarskjöld, the late Secretary General of the United Nations, summed up this kind of life with these words from his book, *Markings,* in which he describes his own spiritual struggle: "In our era, the road to holiness necessarily passes through the world of action."[2]

"He is a good man"—a human being, with faults and weaknesses, but a human being who allows God to work in him. "She is a good woman." She lives so that other people can see something of the love of God and know that, because of her, this world with all its sham, drudgery, darkness, and broken dreams is still a beautiful world.

II

A good person is honest.

What you see is what you get. A good conscience is more than the fear of getting caught. Personal integrity and honesty are still the cement of society.

When personal integrity crumbles, civilization collapses. Today there are signs of alarm. The lack of honesty is a frightening phenomenon.

In my opinion, one of the most sobering comments that emerged from the Watergate scandal in the early 1970s came from the lips of Attorney General John Mitchell. He was the highest law official of the land, and this is how he explained his involvement in the break-in of the Democratic headquarters and the subsequent tampering with the Oval Office tapes: "There is nothing I would not have done to see Richard Nixon elected President."

This is especially frightening because it isn't an isolated comment—it seems to be typical of the way much of our public policy works. During the 1980 presidential campaign, President Carter's debate notes and material were stolen. When all of this came to light a couple of years later and was discussed in the media, I heard a very respected man in government say, "What is all the fuss about? We all know if Reagan's people could get their hands on that kind of material, they would use it. And so would Carter's staff."

And then much more recently, in 1986, the nation was shocked to discover that while President Reagan had been negotiating with America's allies for a strong position against nations which endorse or tolerate terrorism, he had been trading arms to Iran, a supporter of terrorism, in order to effect the release of American hostages in Lebanon. And again there were people who wondered what all the fuss was about. After all, they said, we all wanted the hostages released.

"What's all the fuss about?" Simply that honesty must be a top priority if America is to be the America of our dreams. And this is true of private individuals as well as public figures.

Harry Emerson Fosdick suggested a way to determine our honesty and character—put our behavior to the test of publicity.

What would it be like if everyone knew what you were doing with your life? What if it were stripped of its secrecy and carried into the blazing light of day? How do you feel about those questions? If you know anything about human life, with all its clandestine behavior, you know how authentic a character test that is.

That is not to say, of course, that we must live totally public lives. We all have a stake in preserving privacy in our society. It is not always a healthy act to disclose indiscriminately what we have done and are doing, and there are some actions that by their nature are private. Yet, once that caution is offered, there is something wonderful about living a life in which we have no need of concealment, where we do nothing that couldn't be done in the middle of our own town's city square at midday. That's the glory of a good life.

Charles Swindoll, in *Strengthening Your Grip*, tells an amazing story that highlights this idea. A man went into a fried chicken franchise in Long Beach. The manager inadvertently gave him a chicken box that was full of the previous day's financial receipts. He was going to take the receipts to the bank and he camouflaged it so he wouldn't be robbed. But he gave away the wrong box.

The man went to a park with a young lady for a picnic. As they opened the box they realized that something was amiss. This was a very vulnerable point in this man's life. He said, "Oh, we must be honest." And so the man and his ladyfriend got up, got into the car and went back to the chicken place.

They went in and the manager was thrilled to see them. "It's just wonderful that you've come back. You must stay here. I'll call the newspaper and have a reporter come out and do a story about this. You're the most honest man in town."

The customer said, "No. I don't want you to do that."

"What do you mean you don't want me to do that?"

"I don't want you to do that. You see, I'm married, and the woman I'm with is not my wife."[3]

One way of exploring the issue of character is to ask what we are like when nobody sees us but us. Character is what we are when we don't know anybody is watching us. In such a duplicitous world, that's a good test.

III

A good person knows the power of words and uses them responsibly.

Often we say talk is cheap—words, words, nothing but words. Yet I wonder if there is anything more potent for good or ill than words.

Don't ever call talk cheap. A word makes an indelible impression on the human psyche. Jesus says we should be careful with our speech. In the Sermon on the Mount, there is an astringent passion in Jesus' warning about angry, duplicitous, slanderous words. If you call anyone a fool, he says, or sneer at a person, you will have to answer for it in the fires of hell (Matt. 5:21–22, RSV and NEB).

I don't think we should try to dilute Jesus' passionate judgment of people who plunder another person with words. A word is like a bullet. It leaves its impact on the human tissue and the human psyche no matter what we say.

I watched a small boy being uncooperative and obnoxious in a department store. Finally his father's patience caved in. He lost control of his temper and lashed out at that misbehaving six-year-old, screaming loudly, "You stupid fool, come here."

I could feel the stunned disbelief of people around me as we all felt the psychic waves of the father's angry words. And I grieved for that little boy; what did those words do to his spirit?

And it even occurred to me to wonder what effect those harsh words, "You stupid fool, come here," had on the cosmos! It's something I've thought before. I understand almost every word I speak has a spreading effect, as a pebble makes a ripple in a lake. When I have said a biting, destructive, ugly, angry thing about someone, I have wondered what my angry words do to the creation, to nature, to the very fabric of life.

Perhaps that's too esoteric. Still, we know, through so much demonstrative material, that there is power in words. The tongue is a fire that can inflame a mob to lynch a person or inspire a nation to heroic and generous service. Few words are neutral, and no destructive word can be recalled once it has been spoken. The words we speak either help or hurt someone, and they just might create or destroy parts of the fabric of the cosmos.

As I have mentioned before, I grew up in the restaurant business. My father came to the United States from Patras, Greece, when he was thirteen years old. He was by himself, speaking no English, as he started his way in the new world. Later, his brother, George, joined him, and together they built a great restaurant in Knoxville, Tennessee. Since my mother died when I was five years old, the restaurant was in many ways my home until I went off to seminary.

I remember how the waiters and waitresses had their favorite customers. They were not necessarily the big tippers. They were always the people who in unpatronizing ways had kind, supportive words to offer those who served them.

It is my growing conviction that words of love and kindness have a powerful effect on the nervous system, the heartbeat, the blood pressure—and who knows?—maybe the cosmos itself.

There are many tests for being a good person, but the Bible is clear that one test is the control and use of the tongue: "A man may think he is religious, but if he has no control over his tongue, he is deceiving himself; that man's religion is futile" (James 1:26). Few sins are more heinous than the sin of slander—the defamation of character by distorting the truth. It is an evil, wicked thing to steal someone's honor and integrity by foul and malicious gossip, and retelling a rumor is the same as starting it, for you send it on its damaging way. I believe God will hold us accountable for what we say about people.

The tongue of a person is the clue to the soul—to the inner thoughts, to the character, to the deepest reality of personhood. Do your words about people reveal a beautiful soul?

I am reminded of that poignant saying, "Many have fallen by the edge of the sword, but not as many as have fallen by the tongue." Goodness is that quality that allows us to remember that there is nothing more potent for good or ill than words.

Even our righteous words must be spoken in love if they are to heal rather than injure. I have my faults and weaknesses, my failures and sins, but I hope those who want to speak a word of judgment to me will take on the spirit of Jeremiah, who wept as he spoke the words of judgment.

I often think of that motto I once saw hanging over the fireplace in the den of a home: "Here one speaks of evil only to grieve over it and remedy it." That is goodness.

IV

Goodness is a lifelong process—not an overnight transaction.

No one becomes a good person suddenly, and no one goes to seed overnight. Character is no quick transaction. You are what you have been thinking and doing and dreaming about for a long time.

You grow to be what you are. And that growth can be toward the light or toward the darkness. Growth into goodness is not inevitable!

The graying of a person's hair is a beautiful thing, for it says we've lived and experienced so much of life. But the bleaching of the spirit is a tragedy! There is a loss more deadly than the loss of physical vigor, sadder than the decay of the mental powers—it is the withering of the spirit by an almost imperceptible decline.

The words of the Bible concerning that great hulk of a man, Samson, are terribly disquieting: "He did not know that the Lord had departed from him" (Judg. 16:21, NKJV). He didn't know it, but "prey for seduction" was written all over him, and Delilah took him!

This is one of the reasons, I believe, worship is so critically important. It keeps us focused on the goals of our striving and gives us energy for the journey. The great philosopher Alfred North Whitehead said it best: "Moral education is impossible apart from the habitual vision of greatness." Worship week after week gives us that kind of "habitual vision"—it is that time exposure of the human spirit to the highest we know. We tend inevitably to grow like that to which we give our attention, our admiration, our devotion.

I read of an art gallery where there is an old Greek statue of Apollo, the beautiful figure of physical perfection. Someone visiting the gallery said that he didn't know which was the more impressive—to look at the statue, or to watch the crowd as they looked. Invariably, he said, everyone who stood before the statue, even for a casual instant, began to straighten up, pull back the shoulders, and stand tall.

You can't spend time praying and thinking about Jesus and remain the same. Eventually you will be drawn toward his goodness—a goodness that is beautiful and generous, courageous and strong.

In this lifelong process of growth, it is important deliberately to cultivate our minds with the quality of goodness.

St. Paul, whose world was not much dissimilar to our world, wrote to the church at Philippi, "Finally, brethren, whatever is true, whatever is honorable, whatever is just, whatever is pure, whatever is lovely, whatever is gracious, if there is any excellence, if there is anything worthy of praise, think about these things" (Phil. 4:8). If we want to see goodness permeate this exploited and debased world—a world that is corrupted, a world that's lost hold of the holy—then we need to think on these things.

I believe it is a religious duty to turn our minds daily to what is fine and noble, to be an admirer of those who seek to bring justice and magnificence to life. It is a religious duty to love the highest in human lives when we see it. It is a religious duty to take a hopeful view of the possibilities of life and put our minds squarely against cynicism.

It is a religious duty to remember life at its best moments—a moment when a personal loyalty was able to steady your heart in the midst of a fierce crisis, the moment when your life had depth and excitement because you decided to commit yourself to some great cause, the moment when somehow you sensed the divine presence helping you and a seemingly impossible task got done, the moment when you were moved toward living a more beautiful life because another person believed in you, the moment when you felt the incredible freshness of a new day when the soul was pure and the conscience clean. It is a religious duty to fill your mind with the power of these thoughts.

A love of what is honorable and just and true, even if we only read about it, can inspire an eagerness to emulate it.

And the opposite is true. To have our lives taken up with what is trivial and commonplace is to lose our appetite for what is high and excellent.

We tend inevitably to grow like that to which we give our attention, our thoughts, our admiration, our devotion.

V

Finally, to see goodness in its fullness, we must broaden our concept of what is unacceptably *not good*—what is obscene. In our permissive age, it is easy to point to an increased acceptance in society of nudity and raw language as examples of obscenity. And sometimes these things *are* obscene. But in my mind, the great obscenity of our age is not sexually explicit films, but the way in which we talk so casually about a nuclear holocaust and participate as citizens in decisions that lead almost inevitably to that final day of madness. The great obscenity of our age is not a four-letter word for sex, but the way in which the Western world refuses to release the resources that could end hunger across the planet and save millions of human lives. The great obscenity of our age is not a naked body, but the way in which dignity and honor have been stripped away from people because they are black or brown.

We are called to goodness on a corporate scale, in the decisions we make that affect the well-being of all God's people. We must decide what we will give our lives for, and in that decision we will find God's abiding power to bless us on our way.

The unmaking of Gary Hart as a Democratic presidential candidate in May, 1987, was one of the most startling stories in American politics. A man who had devoted at least four years of his life in eager pursuit of the presidency was undone almost overnight by the revelation of a relationship—chaste or not— with a beautiful twenty-nine-year-old model and actress.

The moral issue of "womanizing" has become central to the American political scene. And understandably so—when honesty and integrity seem at such a premium. But in my opinion, there is another issue at stake here. I feel it would be a mistake to turn the presidential election into keyhole journalism by trying to determine who is sexually pure. Not that sexual behavior isn't part of a person's character formation, not that adultery isn't destructive to a relationship—but a single concentration on personal qualities, especially sexual purity, pushes us toward understanding morality only on a personal level. We are left with a morality—a goodness—that is disconnected from corporate responsibility.

Personal integrity is paramount in the presidency. The lack of honesty in government and throughout American life is a frightening phenomenon. The honor and credibility of the presidency and of all political life are being challenged to the core.

We must have political leaders of strong character if we are to survive as a nation. But character and morality are not private matters alone. A moral person, a good person, is also one who is justly and honorably connected to the whole human family. It is easy to see that a person who steals another person's wallet is a thief and behaves immorally. The person is responsible for her acts. But it is also immoral to steal a person's future by putting a black child in a society that closes doors to her and disadvantages her because of the color of her skin. We are responsible for that, too.

It is a fierce challenge to be a moral person, a good person, in the deepest personal dimensions of life, as well as in our connections with all of God's people.

VI

Goodness is not perfection, but commitment.

Many good people limp because of their sins. They have broken the laws of God and failed the creator of life. Yet they still limp toward the sunrise.

I know these people. They are good people, and God lives in them in power. Goodness is about commitment, not perfection. They have made a decision about what they want to do with their lives, by the grace of God.

C. S. Lewis put it this way: "Each time you make a choice you are turning the central part of you into something different than it was before."

Goodness is that decision not to live in duplicity and dishonor, greed and self-indulgence, apathy and cynicism, vulgarity and obscenity; but in generosity, mercy, purity, tenderness, compassion, and love.

William James, the pioneering psychologist, believed we are free to make such a decision. He said, "With all the pressures on you outside and inside, you have the power to throw your weight on this possibility rather than that. Let this be so!" And this freedom to choose was William James' leap of commitment.

We are called to goodness. That means making a decision about what we want to do with our lives. All of us make a decision about what we are to do with what we are. And all of us *must* decide. Corruption has never been compulsory!

Elie Wiesel tells of an old Jewish legend in which one of God's trusted people goes to the sinful city of Sodom. Night after night he walked the streets, preaching against greed and theft, falsehood and indifference. In the beginning people listened to him and smiled rather ironically. Then they stopped listening. He no longer amused them. The killers went on killing, the thieves went on stealing, the wise kept silent, as if there were no just person in their midst.

One day a child, moved by compassion for the unfortunate preacher, approached him and asked, "Poor stranger, you shout and expend yourself, body and soul. Don't you see it is hopeless?"

"Yes, I see," answered the man.

"Then why go on?"

"I'll tell you why. In the beginning I thought I could save the whole city—change it—but I cannot. Then I thought I could change a few. But now I keep on because I will not let the city ultimately change me."

Goodness is that final commitment to be God's person, no matter what. Not eccentricities, not sanctimoniousness, not withdrawal from the hard life of the world, not perfection—but simply the offer of all that we are to God and to the service of all God's people. That is goodness.

When General William Booth, the founder of the Salvation Army, was dying, one of his associates said to him, "Tell us, General, before you go, what has been the secret of your wonderful life?"

"If there has been any secret," whispered the grand old servant of the world's poor, "it has been that God has had all that there was of me."

That is the high mark, the distinguishing characteristic of goodness in the personal and corporate dimensions of life. How much does God have of you?

VII

You hear the call of God for goodness, but you feel so corrupt. God can deal with you; trust that.

François Mauriac, the Nobel Prize winner for literature, has a little book called *What I Believe*, in which he describes his lifelong search for purity. He says he has come to believe that at the end of life there is no greater happiness than to have loved Christ and been forgiven.

He writes, "You are forgiven. With one single word, one single glance from the Savior, all the wretched abominations of a person's life are obliterated."[4]

We strive for goodness. We want to hold out against the evil forces of the world that would change us. Our desire is to grow more and more into the likeness and stature of Jesus. But our journey into the light is filled with conflicts and failures, so we pray that God's amazing grace—God's merciful forgiveness—will be our companion on the way.

Chapter Eight

Forgiveness: Let's Be
Friends Again

You would be shocked if you really could get a glimpse of the kind of people who followed Jesus around. Jesus was not constrained by all the religious proprieties. He was so confident and secure in God's love that he reached out to everyone. How the failures, the misfits, the nobodies in society loved to be around him! They didn't have to pretend with Jesus. He didn't care for false fronts; he took people just as they were.

These nobodies knew they weren't as good as they should be; nevertheless, Jesus welcomed them—and did they flock to him! Can you imagine how it angered some of the religious authorities and all those proper people to see Jesus mingling with the outcasts of society, going to their homes and eating with them? The air around Jesus must have been electric with their indignation.

There are always some good and proper and respectable people who don't like to think that people who have failed, people who are soiled, deserve respect. In my own home city, there are some who think that the homeless who sleep on our streets and in our alleys are society's failures and should not drain our springs of compassion, let alone our corporate financial resources.

So many people hold distorted ideas of what the Christian community is all about. And in my opinion none is more false or more destructive than the view of a Christian church as the place healthy, normal, well-adjusted, successful people go to have their prosperous well-being blessed by the Almighty.

David Read, the distinguished Presbyterian minister in New York City, once caricatured this view by describing Mr. and Mrs. Normal, who occupy the front pew of a nice, clean church.

Mr. and Mrs. Normal and their two children are dressed nicely, but not too expensively. They look devout, but not too devout. They are singing hymns, but not too lustily.

Mr. and Mrs. Normal obviously fell in love at the right time, had their children at proper intervals, made no mistakes, and experienced no serious problems in their marriage. They are obviously acceptable guests in anyone's home and are members of the country club. They eat without gaining weight and drink without becoming alcoholics and, in matters political, they are always moderate.

The Normal children are growing up without any trouble with the law. They pass their exams at the right time, go to the proper schools, and have the right friends. No drugs or unwanted pregnancies mar the lives of these perfectly adjusted people.

So here are Mr. and Mrs. Normal at church without a worry or concern on their minds. They have come to be blessed for their successful lives. The trouble is—they are a myth! As is a church that is supposed to exist just to bless that normality and inspire all the rest of us to reach this goal.

I know many Christian congregations throughout this nation—and some of them I know intimately. And I am convinced there are few—if any—Mr. and Mrs. Normals. A church is a community of wounded people—men and women with troubled minds and burdened consciences. It is a community in which we are bound together by our brokenness.

Some of us are widows and lonely. Some of us are divorced and bitter. None of us is without frustration. There is a secret battle going on in one heart; some twist of character in another; some agonizing experience of testing in another—all of which cuts us off from that happy picture of Mr. and Mrs. Normal.

Over the years many people have told me how intimidating this picture of the church of Mr. and Mrs. Normal has been to them. They have problems, and the church was never a place that seemed to welcome the broken ones.

What great harm is done when we allow people to think they are the only misfits in the crowd, when actually all around us are Mr. and Mrs. Abnormal. So if we are to live passionate, vital, healthy lives, we must focus on mercy and forgiveness.

The sooner we can explode that myth of the nice, perfectly adjusted Christian, the sooner the broken and wounded ones of the world will come in and share our love.

Remember, the Christian church is the only institution in the world whose qualification for membership is that we be unworthy! So we need to come to terms with sin and forgiveness if we are to find health within a Christian community.

I

We begin with some interpretations of the word *sin.*

I find the story of the prodigal son in Luke 15:11–32 the most illuminating biblical material on sin and forgiveness. And I believe this parable is one of the greatest stories in the world, for everyone's story is a footnote to it.

The younger son took his inheritance and went into a "far country." All of us have felt the lure of the "far country"—the free life. It's so human to want freedom without restraint and rules and obligations, to do as we please and have no one on our backs. He wanted to get rid of all ultimate responsibilities; he wanted to break loose from every tie—even from God. The father could not hold him back. Home would not be home to a boy of alien will.

Yet freedom didn't work out for the boy. The young man's pursuit was illusory, for the basic lie of human existence is that there is liberty without law, freedom without restraint, pleasure without discipline. The prodigal could deny the moral laws of the universe in the far country, but he could not destroy them.

The young man in the story wasted his substance in riotous living, but the sordidness of the parable should not blur its sharpness for us. For there are many types of prodigals, and there are no geographical limits to the far country. We can go astray and waste our substance in many ways other than just becoming a down-and-out drunk or a sexually irresponsible person. Most of us in one way or another find our portrait painted by the divine strokes of the master teacher as he tells of a youth who went into the far country.

There is that glorious moment in the parable when the younger son came to himself and said, "Father, I have sinned, against God and against you; I am no longer fit to be called your son . . ." (v. 18).

"I have sinned. . . ." Do you immediately think of the seventh commandment, "You shall not commit adultery." Or do you envision the prodigal son wasting all his money in reckless living with harlots? We tend to think first of the coarser sins of the flesh.

Much could be said about the sins of the flesh; about glamorized sexual escapades, Hollywood style. Much could be made about the way the media keeps telling us that such sins aren't so bad, that drunkenness isn't anything to be so concerned about, that drugs just help you a little to get through those hard parts of life, and sex—well, anything goes which feels good at the moment. Much could be said about the moral corruption, the disintegration of decency and honor in our society.

And yet when I read those words, "I have sinned," I am quite sure Jesus was not referring only to the wild orgies, the riotous, loose living in which the prodigal had thoroughly indulged himself.

The concept of sin is something deeper and vastly more alarming. It refers to the first commandment, the most important one: "I am the Lord your God who brought you out . . . of slavery. You shall have no other god to set against me" (Exod. 20:3). The essence of sin is disobeying that commandment and refusing to let the Lord God be the God of our lives.

The first commandment establishes our primary loyalty. Either God is to be set at life's center and established as its controlling point, around which all else revolves, or God is not recognized as the Lord God of creation who brings full life.

Martin Luther put it clearly: "I say whatever your heart clings to and confides in, that is really your God."

When the prodigal son finally came to himself and came home, he said, "Father, I have sinned, against God and against you." He was pointing to his deliberate attempt to break his ties, to have no commitments, to have life his own way.

The late Theodore Ferris, the minister who served for so many years at Trinity Episcopal Church, Boston, put it this way: The prodigal's sin was not wasting his substance in the far country, though that was wrong. His sin was that he never wrote home—that he forgot he had a family and belonged to someone.

"I have sinned." That means more than stealing, gambling, drinking, sleeping around. It means leaving home without caring, cutting yourself off from those who gave you life, cutting yourself off from the cradle of your existence. "I have sinned"—that means trying to live as though you had no home, no God, no one but yourself to be responsible to.

The lusts which cause us to exploit our sexuality, the jealousies that poison so many lovely relationships, the bitternesses that disfigure friendship, the compromises that discredit us, the lack of willpower that enchains us, the duplicity that dishonors us, the cowardice that humiliates us—all the misery and the pain of life, says the biblical tradition, stem from the quintessential sin of leaving our true home, of replacing the Lord God on the throne and centering life upon ourselves.

There is a Danish fable which tells how a spider slid down a single filament of web from the lofty timbers of a barn and established himself on the lower level. There he spread his web, caught flies, grew sleek, and prospered. One Sunday afternoon, wandering about his premises, he saw the thread that stretched up into the dark unseen above him and thought, "How useless!" He snapped it. But then his web collapsed and soon he was trodden underfoot.

When we organize life around ourselves and cut the cord that keeps us in touch with God, the source of existence, we fall, and great is the fall.

II

The prodigal son went home to his father's forgiveness.

Just as there is deep in human nature a leaning toward a destructive self-centeredness, there is also a deep-seated homing instinct.

The prodigal son wanted to leave home and live life on his own terms, and this he did. But he came to himself and knew this was not what life was meant to be. He wanted to go home to be with his family again, for he had discovered he could have no real life cut off from them.

"Father, I have sinned against God and against you." He refused to excuse himself. He was broken by his sin and acknowledged it. With tears on his cheeks and pain in his heart, the prodigal cried out, "Father, I have sinned." That was the beginning of new life.

Do not be sad that you have a deep, heavy sorrow over some moral failure in your past. Repentance is the cry within us for new life and authentic fulfillment. In a poem by Thomas Moore, a person is charged with going to earth from heaven to search for the world's greatest treasure. He finally returns with a tear of repentance, which proves to be the most precious thing that the earth can produce.

Some of us remember the bitter taste of a life in a "far country" and the pain it produced in our souls. And some of us know that our sorrow and repentance opened the door for God to create a new life. M. L. Sullivan says it best: "There is in repentance this beautiful mystery—that we fly fastest home on a broken wing."

The prodigal son came home to the father's love and mercy. The father in the story—who could ever forget this welcome?—came rushing out to meet the wayward son. The son tried to get out his confession—"Father, I've sinned against God and you, and I'm not worthy to be called a son . . ."—but the father would not listen to any of it. There in the middle of the road he embraced his son and kissed away his confession.

The son expected the worst—to be a paid servant in his

father's house. That would be justice. He deserved no better. The very best he could have hoped for was a harsh reproach, a setting of the son apart from the family till he proved his sincerity. But no, there was no reproach, no trial period—only the fullness of a father's love, which was greater than justice.

Then there was a party to celebrate the son's return. "Quick! fetch a robe, my best one, and put it on him; put a ring on his finger and shoes on his feet. Bring the fatted calf and kill it, and let us have a feast to celebrate the day. For this son of mine was dead and has come back to life; he was lost and is found" (vv. 22–24).

I wonder if there has ever been a more dynamic, more explosive idea urged into human thought than Christ's insistence that God is like that parent. I wonder if there has ever been a more hope-giving declaration put into the hearts of people than Jesus' insistence that we can go home and be forgiven.

Greta Garbo once confessed to an interviewer, "I've made a mess of my life." Some of us know what she meant, for most of us have been in one far country or another and strayed from God's ways.

We desperately want the chance to try again. We want to come home to love and a new beginning. And the central reality of the life and spirit of Jesus is that this hope is possible!

The brilliant theologian Paul Tillich said that nothing greater can happen to a human being than to be forgiven. This is true, but persistent questions surround such a statement. What do we do when we forgive someone? What do we receive when we are forgiven by someone? What happens between two people when one forgives and the other is forgiven? And does it take a miracle to pull it off?

III

There are two things that forgiveness does not mean.

Forgiveness does not cancel out the consequences of our sins. The mistakes and failures and disloyalties of the past

leave their mark on us and those around us. The prodigal son
was forgiven, but the joy of his father's love did not blot out
the son's memory of his life in the far country among the
swine. The father's mercy did not undo the consequences of
the son's dishonor. We suffer for the evil we do.

> The Moving Finger writes; and, having writ,
> Moves on: nor all thy Piety nor Wit
>   Shall lure it back to cancel half a Line,
> Nor all thy Tears wash out a Word of it.[1]

The prodigal son was forgiven, but his past left its marks
on him, and the father's mercy could not blot them out.

If we waste our talents and misuse our bodies, if we yield
habitually to deceit and fray the invisible fibers of loyalty
that bind us to a community, if we soil the innocence of others
and trample upon their integrity, if we break that precious
trust of a spouse, if we renege on a friendship in order to
promote our own position and status, if we willingly afflict
and abuse a child of God, if we betray a friend who trusts us
by gossiping to others, if we violate the realities of the universe that draw us toward peace and justice and reconciliation, then these moral wrongs will leave their mark on us.
Forgiveness does not annul the consequences of our actions.

The prodigal son had to face the scars of the past in his
own life and in the lives of the loved ones he had hurt. The
story is told that on the morning after his return home,
the prodigal son arose late, fatigued by the long journey home
and the late night celebration. He went out into the bright
sunlight of the field where his father was working and saw for
the first time that his father's hair had turned white! We can
be forgiven, but those mistakes and failures and disloyalties
leave their marks somewhere, and all the tears of repentance
cannot wash them completely away.

Second, forgiveness does not mean forgetting. A husband
said to his wife after an argument, "Come now, I thought you
had agreed to forgive and forget." "Yes," she replied, "but I
don't want you to forget that I have forgiven and forgotten!"

Forgiveness is not forgetting. Lewis Smedes writes in his fascinating and extremely helpful book, *How Can It Be All Right When Everything Is All Wrong?*:

> Forgetting is not hard and it is not painful. We forget what does not matter much for us anyway. You need no miracle of grace to get you to forget. All you need is a bad memory, or maybe a fear of reality so intense that you stuff the ugly pain of the past into the dark pit of your unconscious.[2]

So the hurts we do forget are those too trivial to remember.

I find the common linkage between forgiving and forgetting very unhealthy and destructive. The memories of hurt and disloyalty are not quickly banished. We know that it takes time and grace to heal those painful memories—and they are not healed when they are repressed and forgotten.

Forgiveness is not forgetting. Rather, forgiveness is re-membering and still forgiving! That is the miracle of grace—to wince at the memory of a hurtful act, yet to forgive and be reconciled. As the years go on, the grace of God does work at those deep levels in healing the memories.

In his book, *Forgive and Forget,* Dr. Smedes writes:

> We all wish at one time that we could reach back to a painful memory and cut it out of our lives. Some people are lucky; they seem to have gracious glands that secrete the juices of forget-fulness. They never hold a grudge; they do not remember old hurts. Their painful yesterdays die with the coming of tomor-row. But most of us find that the pains of our past keep rolling through our memories and there is nothing we can do to stop the flow.[3]

Nothing? Smedes points to a way out. The only power that can stop the inexorable stream of painful memories is the "faculty of forgiveness"—which heals the memories rather than causes us to forget.

Jesus came to show us the power of forgiveness. Forgive-ness is God's invention for coming to terms with a world in which people are unfair to each other and hurt each other deeply. God began by forgiving us and he invites us to forgive each other.

IV

If forgiveness is not the cancellation of the consequences of our failures and mistakes—if it is not forgetting the hurt of these disloyalties—then what is it?

Forgiveness is a new beginning—the restoration of a relationship. At bottom, forgiveness is this simple sort of miracle, starting over and trying again with a person who caused you pain. It is a welcome home.

God does that when God forgives us. God offers us a new start. No matter what it is that we have done, God holds out a hand and says, "Come on, take it; I want to be your friend again. In spite of everything I want to be around you and in you and be the power of your existence. I am not going to let anything you do get in my way. So let's begin again."

That's what God does in forgiveness. And it is exactly what we do with each other when we forgive. We start not where we wish we were, but right where we are in the midst of all the pain, and we hold out our hand and say, "I want to be your friend again. I want to be your mother again . . . your daughter again . . . your lover again. Let's start over."

That is forgiveness. The past, with all its pain, is there; we can't change it. But forgiveness means the past is not held against the future.

A young woman deceives her father and hurts him deeply. She takes a trust and soils it and dishonors a man who loves her so much. There is something broken between them. When she comes to herself, she asks to be forgiven. She is not thinking of getting off scot-free for the harm she has done. She knows her father may remember her betrayal for years. Yet forgiveness means the deceitful act shall no longer separate them. It means a new beginning, and they shall reach across that chasm of estrangement and be to each other what they were before the offense was committed.

What that young woman has done to her father can't be

undone; only time and grace will heal the scars. But he can will that the past not be held against her future—that is the grace of forgiveness.

V

This message of forgiveness needs to go into those deep places of our hearts and spirits, for all of us want it for ourselves. There are two things we need to do if we are to know the healing power of forgiveness.

First, we must acknowledge our need for forgiveness—for this new beginning, this future where the past is no longer held against us.

We must acknowledge that in some ways we have gone astray and life isn't going well for us. We must acknowledge that we have taken God off the altar and put in God's place success at any cost or happiness at any price or our country right or wrong. We must acknowledge that our lives aren't the authentic ones we know God wants us to have; they are bleak and empty. We must tell God that we are tired of the far country and we want to come home.

No forgiveness and healing are possible if we don't know we need it. There is a story of a woman who was having her portrait painted. When it was finished, she complained, "It doesn't do me justice." The artist replied, "It isn't justice you need, lady, but mercy!" So do we all.

The inability to repent is probably the worst imprisonment any person can experience. It locks us into the old bleak world. Repentance gives us freedom to turn around and start life all over again.

I love people who willingly accept their frailties—their mistakes, their errors, even their idolatries. If we don't accept such things—recognize them and take hold of them—then we become hard. And worst of all, what we often find wrong in another person is the very fault we don't want to face in ourselves. The best thing I've found to do with my mistakes and failures is to admit them and then get on with life.

There is an old story of a man who stopped at a country

store to ask the distance to a certain town. The reply was, "If you continue in the direction you are going, it will be about twenty-five thousand miles, but if you turn around, it will be about three miles." Repentance means the freedom to turn around and come home to God and to your true self. The acknowledgment that I am a sinner is glorious, for it leads me to forgiveness and new life.

That's all any of us has to do—acknowledge our sins, confess, "God, I have sinned against you and my sisters and brothers of the world." We don't have to win favor with God, nor plead with God, nor cajole God to gain forgiveness.

The door of divine mercy is wide open; the nail-pierced hands of Jesus opened it. You and I can walk through it. Forgiveness does not wait for us to reform before it is offered.

God's loving acceptance is offered to us just as we are. All we must do is take it. That is grace—amazing grace.

Remember that every saint has a past and every sinner has a future! That's what repentance and forgiveness are all about.

The second requirement if you are to be forgiven is this: You must forgive yourself and others.

Forgiveness is limitless; nothing is beyond God's mercy to redeem—nothing. But forgiveness is conditional. There is a toughness in God's love. God doesn't put up with our receiving forgiveness and refusing to pass it on.

God's forgiveness is simply the opportunity to start a new life. But you must ratify that forgiveness; you must root it down in your soul by passing it on. All that God's mercy has done for us becomes an indictment on us if we don't let it flow through us to others. Bottle up this divine mercy all for ourselves and it becomes a poison to the spirit rather than the miracle of life.

One day I was talking to a man who had been divorced for many years. In that conversation he revealed, with deep anguish, that he and his former wife had never spoken to each other since their separation many years ago. "She just won't talk to me," he said. "We communicate through the kids." Oh, I'm sure that man had made terrible mistakes and hurt that woman deeply. But the kind of hatred she showed him bars us from the love of the God that can give us new life and new hope. She was imprisoned by her bitterness.

Do you ever wonder how God puts up with us? We've failed God so often. How God must weary of us. And yet, God loves us and offers us new life and hope.

When people heap harsh criticism and condemnation on others or persist in running themselves down, I wonder if they have forgotten—or ever known—how mercifully God treats them. For when we remember how badly we've messed up life—and yet how mercifully God has treated us—then our hearts are softer and our compassion embraces people with kindness.

Many years ago Morton Thompson's novel, *Not As a Stranger,* was a bestseller. It is the story of Lucas Marsh, an ambitious young doctor whose own brilliance and capability have made him impatient and intolerant of everyone, even his wife.

On one occasion he goes to the president of the district medical association to accuse an older colleague of malpractice and to request that the man's license to practice medicine be revoked.

The president listens to the young doctor patiently, then asks him to reconsider his charges. He suggests that Dr. Marsh should not act hastily, but should remember that any person in the zealousness of youth judges more harshly than after he has mellowed with age and experience. He also says that all doctors make honest mistakes, that no one is perfect.

Marsh remains adamant, however, so the president adopts a different attitude. He leans forward across his desk and says, "I am going to suggest this to you—that if you persist in bringing formal charges, don't ever make a mistake." He paused. The words crashed down again: "Don't you ever—as long as you live—make a single mistake."[4]

Remember that the one who cannot forgive and show mercy has destroyed the bridge over which she someday must travel.

Bitterness is so corrupting to the soul—such a dissipater of power! The people who are alive with vitality—the beautiful people, the ones who captivate and inspire us—are invariably people who refuse to harbor bitterness in their souls.

I worked for several years with a woman who was painfully crippled with rheumatoid arthritis. She also had the most bitter, vitriolic attitude toward her mother I'd ever encountered. Sometimes her expressions of hatred and contempt stunned me and left me breathless.

Fortunately, this woman's physician saw the causal connection between her deep-seated bitterness and her sickness. After almost two years of counseling with me and some long conversations together with her wise physician, she let go of the hatred and vindictiveness that were poisoning her system. Her mother had hurt her profoundly and damaged her psyche. There was cause for her antagonism. Yet she finally confessed to God that her bitter hatred toward this woman was also alienating her from God. She released it all to God and allowed God's grace to cleanse and restore her life. Within a year she was a healthy, whole person.

Forgiveness leads you to health. As long as you hold on to your bitterness—to some past dirt someone has done to you—your spirit is corrupted and your body takes the rap. When you hold a person accountable for his or her behavior but then forgive the person for all the torture and pain he or she brought into your life, you then release yourself from the tyranny of vengeance. When you forgive that person, you walk out of the prison of pain into the light.

The most beautiful people I know have this grace of forgiveness at the center of their lives.

A family lost their only son in the Vietnam war and said this: "We don't hate anyone. We just can't bear to think of adding any more grief and suffering to the world." That is the spirit that leads to healing, for it is in tune with the intention of life's creator and redeemer.

VI

Focus on forgiveness—for the wonder of wonders is that God's forgiveness gives you the opportunity to start life all over again.

Rebirth always happens at the moment when we let go of yesterday's failures and embrace today's hopes, when we know the past will not be held against our future, when, in spite of everything, we reach again for the hand of a friend.

Early in my ministry, when I was living in Tennessee, I heard J. Wallace Hamilton tell a story which lodged itself deep into my mind. Again and again, that story has helped to renew my hope in the possibilities of new life. Over the years I've heard the tale told by different people in a variety of forms—but thirty years ago, I heard Dr. Hamilton tell it, and it has stayed central to my thinking.

Dr. Hamilton said he was traveling on a train through Florida and noticed a young boy across the aisle from him. The boy was nervous, fidgety, tense, restless. He would sit in one seat and then quickly move to another.

"What's troubling you, friend?" Dr. Hamilton asked.

"Sure, I don't mind telling you. The next stop is Springvale, and we'll be there in fifteen minutes. My mother and father still live there just three miles this side of town in a small farmhouse.

"Three years ago I had a horrible quarrel with my father and ran away from home. I said, 'You'll never see me again!' Three years—and what rough years! I occasionally wrote my mother, and last week I told her I'd be on a train passing through Springvale. And I said I'd like to come home just once. I asked her, if it was all right for me to stop, just to hang something white outside the farmhouse. Then I would know that my father had agreed to let me stop.

"I told her not to do it unless my father agreed. She would let me regardless, but I had to know how Dad felt about it."

The boy looked out the window. "Look, sir, my house is just around the bend, beyond this hill. Oh, what if there is not something white on the farmhouse?"

The train made the slow curve, and Hamilton kept his eye on the round of the hill. Then he shouted, "Look, look, there it is!"

There stood the farmhouse under the trees. You could hardly see the house for all the white. It was ablaze in white. It looked as though his mother and father had taken every bedsheet, every tablecloth, every pillowcase—everything they owned that was white—and hung it on the clothesline and the trees.

And the boy's face went white. He clutched his old, cheap suitcase and was out of the train before it had fully stopped. "I'll never forget," Hamilton said, "that boy running up the hill to the house where the white sheets fluttered in the wind."

Amazing grace—the doors of the universe are open to the possibilities of new life.

Chapter Nine

Joy: Bear a Burden and Find a Joy

In a recent mental health survey, only 20 percent of the people in America interviewed said they enjoyed life and were happy.

An informal survey of counselors would tell you that for many people Christmas is one of the most painful times of the year. The expectations for happiness are so great, yet the sense of inner joy is frequently absent.

"Joy to the world," we sing. But many of us have not gotten hold of that joy and, furthermore, we don't see any way out of this valley of gloom.

And yet . . . the passionate, healthy, vital life is a joyous one. So how do we get hold of that joy that is powerful enough to lift us out of the bleak valleys of life and sustain us with a new quality of living?

I

Joy is an inside job.

It grows out of one's relationship with one's self, with other people, with the universe, with God; it's that interior quality that brings joy.

A man was very despondent and sought the help of a counselor. The counselor listened to his problem and then suggested that the man go and listen to a famous comedian who was in town that particular week. "He will make you laugh and bring some joy to your life. He can dispel the darkness from your heart, for he is able to make the crowds roar." There was silence until the man said, "I am that comedian." He knew it took more than another person's joy to lift the bleakness from his spirit. It had to come from the depths within himself.

Real joy is not externally produced. That's the reason it can exist in the midst of our sadness. And that's because joy is inside; it is the expression of our faith that God is with us no matter what happens and will never desert us; it is the fruit of the spirit of God living deeply within us. So joy comes from inner peace and not from outer security. It is the result of spiritual blessing and not material attainment. It is something we do within ourselves and not something done for us.

The people who are alive with joy and vitality, the beautiful people, the ones who captivate and inspire us, are invariably people who refuse to harbor bitterness in their souls.

Desmond Tutu, the Archbishop of Cape Town, South Africa, is one of my heroes—one of the great lights on the world scene today. Few things in my life have thrilled my heart more than the news that Desmond Tutu had been awarded the Nobel Peace Prize. The black voice that wins the broadest acceptance among blacks in South Africa today belongs to this irrepressible Anglican Archbishop. He is constantly in and out of serious trouble because of his denunciation of the government's policy of apartheid—the strict separation of races. Again and again the government has taken away his passport, for he refuses to remain silent in the face of such institutionalized evil—the brutal dehumanization of his black sisters and brothers.

In South Africa, an eighteen-year-old white person can vote, while this fifty-six-year-old bishop, educated at King's College, London, is barred because of the biological irrelevancy of a black skin. Yet Archbishop Tutu is robust, irrepressible, witty, full of joy and fun. "People ask me why I laugh so much," he said. "It's because I'm on the winning side. God rules! Destroy Tutu, but God goes on. God's justice is unstoppable."

I spent some time with Archbishop Tutu in Johannesburg while I was on a sabbatical in 1978. I've read his books, heard him speak many times over the years, and had the wonderful experience of having him spend a weekend with us at All

Saints Church in Pasadena. In my mind, the most remarkable quality of this man is his heart-wrenching love and forgiveness toward those who persecute and attempt to destroy the black leadership in South Africa. He said, "I will not allow bitterness to enter my soul. They are God's children too."

What amazing grace! One sees the divine light in Desmond Tutu. It is not tarnished by hatred. And so his joy is genuine.

I spent two weeks in the summer of 1984 on a fact-finding trip to El Salvador and Nicaragua. To me, the deepest religious experience of that trip to Central America was meeting Commandante Tomas Borge, one of the founders of the Sandinista Front, which in 1979 overthrew the Somoza government in Nicaragua. Unquestionably, the Sandinista revolution is severely flawed, but my experience is that it has brought hope and a better life to the poor of that land. And in my mind the good aspects of the revolution are summed up by the generous spirits of men like Tomas Borge.

Commandante Borge spent twelve years in jail under Somoza and saw his wife and three-year-old daughter killed by Somoza's national guard. Yet this tough old man told us he believes passionately in prayer, for it purifies the soul from bitterness. For him the greatest virtues are generosity and self-sacrifice.

After the triumph of the Sandinistas over Somoza, the new government called for humane treatment of the ex-national guardsmen who had been taken prisoners. "As much as two years before the triumph," Borge says, "we were afraid that after Somoza was gone there would be a popular reaction that we could not control. We feared that people would take justice in their own hands and take revenge for so many grievances they had suffered for so many years. We were trying to help people look upon generosity as a great virtue. Few revolutions do that. Most try to help the people understand why mass killings and mass executions are required."

Those words were simply overwhelming to me in a world so permeated with violence and greed and retaliation.

"So why did we make this revolution," said Commandante Tomas Borge, who had suffered so much, "if we are going to do the same things they used to do? . . . We are going to be different." Those were the words he spoke before an angry crowd determined to execute former Somoza guardsmen.

I've prayed a lot since meeting Borge that God will let such a spirit grow in me—that God will plant and nurture that virtue of generosity in my heart. In the end it is the only thing that will triumph, the only thing that will bring joy to my soul. I've also prayed that through many of us who believe in self-determination of Nicaragua, something of this generosity of spirit could enter those who make the policies of our nation toward Nicaragua.

Desmond Tutu and Tomas Borge are vastly different people. But each has a mission. Each wants to give back to life something rich and powerful. Maybe Leo Rosten was right when he said, "The purpose of life is simply to count, to matter, to make a difference that you lived at all." That cannot possibly be done if we allow bitterness to soil our souls.

Every one of us today has a history; we've been hurt in the past. But whatever that history is, it's gone—it's past. We must love it, embrace it, and forgive it in the power of Jesus. We will always be unable to choose life now—a life that is beautiful and rich and joyous and full—until we learn to forgive. We must forgive people who have done ill to us. We must say to them, "It it all right; it is over—buried and forgiven." If we don't, then we carry all those weights around our necks like dead albatrosses, and they weigh us down.

As we saw in the previous chapter, forgiveness does not mean forgetting. How could Desmond Tutu possibly forget what the whites have done to him and to his black brothers and sisters in South Africa? In our hearts we know that only time and grace will heal those painful memories.

Forgiveness is not forgetting. Rather, forgiveness is remembering and still forgiving.

When you learn to forgive, you then can cut those heavy weights free, and all those energies you use to keep things in check can then be used to help you grow and become beautiful.

I sense that these two men I have described to you are too

great to be soiled by bitterness. Despite all the cruelty they have undergone for the things they believe in with all the fiber of their beings, they have found the amazing grace to be generous. And in the process they have opened the way for abundant joy in their lives.

II

Joy is now.

"Awake, sleeper, rise . . . and Christ will shine upon you" (Eph. 5:14). "Behold, now is the acceptable time; now is the day of salvation" (2 Cor. 6:2, RSV). "I offer you the choice of life or death, blessing or curse. Choose life and then you and your descendants will live" (Deut. 30:19). "Choose this day whom you will serve" (Joshua 24:15, RSV). There is an urgency in the Bible that is unmistakable.

There is only one time to live—not in the past glories or the future hopes—but in the present moment. Live now or you will never really live at all.

In that homespun play, *Our Town*, Thornton Wilder probes with devastating power to alert us to the preciousness of every passing moment of life.

Remember Emily's poignant words? "It goes so fast. We don't have time to look at one another. . . . Oh earth," she cries, "you're too wonderful for anyone to realize you." Then she asks abruptly through her tears, "Do any human beings ever realize life while they live it?—every, every minute?"[1]

Elisabeth Kübler-Ross, who has written extensively on death and dying, tells us that the people who scream the loudest on their deathbeds are those who have never really lived. They've been the observers of life, but not active participants. They've taken no risks. They stood on the sidelines.

Death tells us our time on earth is limited. To miss the present moment is to miss life.

Parents frequently ask me if they should bring children to funerals. And my view is that we should be honest with children about death and include them in the rituals associated with death. We do them no favor by giving them the impression we all live forever.

Sigmund Freud said so many of our problems and our inability to live and love stem from the belief that we will never die, that we have forever. I believe he is right. Living closely to one's own death can bring intensity and vitality to life, because we are constantly aware that this moment is all we may have.

What time do you have? Is your clock set in the past or the future? Or do you live now—this present moment? Oh yes, let memories of the past strengthen you, and let hope in the future's possibilities encourage you, but the time to live is now, the present moment.

Some of us spend a lifetime preparing to live and never make it. I love the novelist James Michener's comment, "Don't put off for tomorrow what you can do today, because if you enjoy it today, you can do it again tomorrow!"

What time do you have? Isn't it strange how unwelcome the present moment often is? Maybe it's 9:00 A.M. on Monday and we look forward to 5:00 P.M. on Friday. Maybe we think life will really begin when we get that college degree we missed when we were young. Maybe we think when we find another job or another spouse, our life will be more bearable. Maybe there will be a golden time out there somewhere when there are no pressures on us, when we don't have to work so hard, when life isn't rushed and we can do all the wonderful things that we've postponed so long.

A life postponed is a wasted life. Beneath all those refusals to take the present moment and live it is the ticking of the clock. A second ago I was stepping into college with my heart full of hopes and my mind full of dreams. Today I am a grandfather. A person lives now or never lives at all.

I am fully aware of the serious problems presented by the instant gratification syndrome of our culture. Yet I am convinced that the adult propensity to postpone life is an even more severe problem.

The deepest sorrows of life are not in death itself but in what dies in people while they still live.

A preacher once saw his town placarded with notices that a minister of a very ardent nearby church was to address his congregation on the subject, "Millions now living shall never die." He countered the publicity the next week by announcing that he would preach on the subject, "Millions now living are already dead."

He is right. There are lots of people who have lost life and still walk around the streets. Vitality and vigorous life have nothing to do with years. I know some thirty-year-old men walking around who are already dead—they just haven't fallen over yet. I love that epitaph on the tomb which read, "Here lies one who died at thirty and was buried at seventy."

I once read the following reflections of an unknown friar who no doubt was approaching the end of his life. The man's response is magnificent:

If I had my life to live over, I'd try to make more mistakes next time. I would relax, I would limber up; I would be sillier than I have been on this trip. I know of very few things I would take seriously. I would be less hygienic. I would take more chances. I would take more trips. I would climb more mountains, swim more rivers and watch more sunsets. I would eat more ice cream. I would have more actual troubles and fewer imaginary ones.

You see, I am one of those people who lives prophylactically and sensibly and sanely, hour after hour, day after day. Oh, I have had my moments and, if I had it to do over again, I'd have more of them. In fact, I'd try to have nothing else. Just moments, one after another, instead of living so many years ahead each day.

I've been one of those people who never go anywhere without a thermometer, a hot water bottle, a gargle, a raincoat, and a parachute. If I had it to do over again, I would go places and do things and travel lighter than I have . . . but you see, I don't.

Oh, live life today. Actor Robin Williams put it this way: "The greatest gift is life; the biggest sin is to return it unopened." This incredible, beautiful, challenging life is God's gift to you. The way you live your life is your gift to God and your way to authentic, powerful joy.

III

Joy is the byproduct of a holy life.

Joy awaits those who dare to live life as God intends it—in the spirit of Jesus, feeding the hungry, forgiving the offenders, bringing peace and justice, caring for strangers, reconciling difficult people.

Surprised by Joy is the title C. S. Lewis gave his autobiographical reflections. It hints at the way we come by deep, abiding joy. For joy is not to be found by direct pursuit. Rather, in the pursuit of high goals, worthy causes, eternal values, righteous living, one is surprised by joy. It comes along in the parentheses!

Life will be happy and successful, I believe, only if we live with the grain of the universe—as creation has destined us. And we are created in such a way that our lives work beautifully only when we seek and learn how to serve. That is the way to a joy the world can never take away. To grow a life that is beautiful, you must learn to give it away.

Those who live passionately know that life's meaning isn't found in what we get out of life, but in what we put into it. George Bernard Shaw put it this way: " I am of the opinion that my life belongs to the whole community, and so long as I live, it is my privilege to do for it whatever I can. I want to be thoroughly used up when I die."

I will guarantee you something. The only way you will be a vigorous and passionate and lovely person twenty years from now is to pick up some great burdens to bear for God and for God's human family.

It's such a miracle, but I've seen it happen too many times to doubt it. One bears a burden and finds joy. One soothes the wounds of a broken world and finds one's life healed.

In Arthur Miller's play, *The Death of a Salesman,* Willy Loman's wife cannot understand why he should have committed suicide. She says, "At this time especially. First time in thirty-five years we were just about free and clear. He only needed a little salary. He was even finished with the dentist."

But a friend says wisely, "No man needs only a little salary."[2]

When a person's dreams and goals and purposes are destroyed, life goes, too. "A man needs more than a little salary." We all need some dream to which we can give ourselves— something bigger than ourselves.

Let those wild dreams Jesus put forth by the biblical message be in your heart: a land of beauty and loveliness, a society where none live in fear and all are free to be who they are, a human family which is reconciled and among which no one hungers anymore, a world community where war in all its insanity and death is renounced forever.

If we want joy for our lives, we must take on some hard work for the sake of God's kingdom. If we give our lives away to those dreams of the biblical message, we will find them given back enriched and transformed.

We all need something to work for outside ourselves— something bigger than we are. The unhappiest people I know are the ones who never escape the prisons of the self, who never find a cause worthier than their own frets and ailments, and who think the world should devote itself to making them happy. William Sloane Coffin of Riverside Church says, "The smallest package in the world is a person all wrapped up in himself."

A large number of people in this generation have tested the absolute limits of a life lived for self, for personal gratification—a life without commitment. And as far as I can make out, this search for happiness through personal gratification has worked well only for the tranquilizer industry!

We need to take upon our hearts and minds a share of the burden of pain that lies upon the world. We need to allow our hearts to be broken by the things that break the heart of God. Then we begin to move toward the center of our existence, where God gives us life that is full and rich, with a meaning the world cannot give or ever take away.

If you hoard your life, you lose it. If you give it away, it comes back rich and transformed. Jesus said this over and over again. It is a truth woven into the fabric of the universe.

Too many religious people miss this central truth of the Bible. Yet the Bible is clear and unambiguous: a religion that does not turn us toward our brothers and sisters of the world so we can help to alleviate the misery of human life is simply false.

Nothing is more blighting to the life of a church than merely splashing about in a liturgy—however gloriously it is said or sung—if we fail to live the life toward which those words and symbols direct us. Dietrich Bonhoeffer, who died in a concentration camp for his opposition to Hitler, put it boldly in his own context: "Only those who cry for the Jews can sing Gregorian chants."

I am keenly aware of the large numbers of people who come to a church community with great burdens on their hearts and deep distress in their spirit. Life can be hard and cruel, and many of us come to a church seeking comfort and relief; we come seeking a God who can bind up our broken hearts. Yet I want to proclaim to you the biblical truth that is deeply rooted in my mind and heart: your participation in meeting the needs of your brothers and sisters of the world is an absolute prerequisite to your gaining life's deepest meaning. I've seen it too many times to doubt it.

Several years ago, a woman and her husband came to our worship celebration as visitors. On her first visit, the woman told me she was dying of cancer. They continued to come week after week.

One Sunday I preached on the madness of the arms race and our basic obligations as faithful stewards to preserve the planet from a nuclear holocaust. I stated my conviction that God's call is for us to work for a reordering of our national priorities so that the poor and the sick might be healed and have a chance for abundant life.

This dear woman asked me at the door of the church if she could talk to me a minute when I was finished greeting people. I agreed to it, but I was a little apprehensive. That kind of prophetic sermon is always hard to preach because I do know something of the burdens and heartaches people carry, and I feared that I had not ministered well to this woman. Maybe she had come for bread and I had given her a stone.

But she surprised me. "As you know, I have had cancer for a number of years," she said. "Now I am worse, and I know I'm dying. I want a church that believes in healing the body and soul. I think you do. But what's more important to me is that you all at All Saints seem to be concerned about healing the world and caring for the desperate ones. Deep down inside I know I am tied up in the destiny of all God's four billion children and my health ultimately depends on the health of all people. I hope you'll take me in as a member of this church."

This woman was so beautiful and so alive! She knew that if she said "my life" rather than "our life" she would lose it all. She believed that God had created the world in such a way that it only works for those who share life and find their destinies tied up in the destiny of the whole creation.

I know only one kind of funeral that is truly tragic. It is the funeral of a person who has never lived—never lived passionately and vulnerably. When people die without ever really giving their lives away for the world, having thought only of their own lives and careers, never of the common good—that is disaster. When people die never having known the ecstatic joys of forgiving and bridging great estrangements—that is desolation. When people die without having created within their own souls something worthy of eternity—that is failure.

I can still hear those eloquent words of Martin Luther King, Jr., ringing in my ears. He walked constantly with death and finally fell victim to an assassin's bullet, but he said, "Oh, the worst of all tragedies is not to die young but to live until I am seventy-five and yet not ever truly to have lived."

I remember how Henry Thoreau said, "Oh, God, to have reached the point of death only to find that you have never lived!" Yes, that's tragedy. But to take the risks of giving life away, to share the destiny of the human family, to affirm our

solidarity with our brothers and sisters of the world and say
"our life" rather than "my life"—that is to be alive with passion and vitality.

There is a classic story about a woman who died and was
sent to eternal torment. In her agony she cried for mercy. At
last an angel answered, "I can help you only if you can remember one totally unselfish thing you did while on earth."

It seemed easy at first, but when she started reciting her
good deeds, they all seemed to be done out of self-interest.
Finally, at the point of despair, she remembered an onion she
had once given a beggar. She hated to mention it because it
had been a poor withered onion that she would have never
used in the stew she was preparing. But the angel consulted
the record, and it showed that the act had indeed been
prompted by unselfishness. It was not great unselfishness.
She could have given much more. But this much she had
given to help someone else.

So down the limitless space that separates heaven from
hell, the onion was lowered on a slender string. Could this
weak thing bear her weight and lift her out of the torment? It
did not seem possible, but desperation made her try. She
grasped the withered onion and slowly began to rise.

Then she felt a weight dragging at her feet. She looked
down and saw other tormented souls clinging to her, hoping
to escape with her.

"Let go! Let go!" the woman cried. "The onion won't hold
all of us." But grimly, desperately, they held on as the onion
lifted them all toward heaven.

Again she cried, "Let go! This is my onion." At that point the
string broke. And still clutching the onion she had claimed all
for herself, the woman fell back into the torment of hell.

Deep, authentic joy comes when we live in congruence with
the purposes of God's creation and share our life with others.

Part Four

The Vast Implications

Chapter Ten

You Must Kiss Yourself

Can you identify with Charles Schulz's character in this *Peanuts* cartoon?

Charlie Brown is lamenting his lifelong sense of insecurity. "It goes all the way back to the beginning," he says. "The moment I was born and stepped on the stage of history, they took one look at me and said, 'Not right for the part!'"

Lots of people just don't feel good about themselves. Karen Horney, the noted psychiatrist, has suggested that "one's basic anxiety about oneself" is the main barrier to healthy life. And that anxiety is deep within us; it responds to no simple solution.

We humans are creatures wonderfully made—but creatures full of paradoxes. We believe and doubt, love and hate, hope and despair; we are exciting and boring, manic and depressive. We feel good, and we feel guilty about feeling good. We are cool on the outside but hurt down deep within. We think we have all the answers, and we feel the foundations of certainty are slipping from beneath our feet. We are trusting and suspicious. We are honest, and we play games with life. We are open and vulnerable, but part of us is locked up tight. We thrill with joy at a baby's birth, and we store up resentment in our hearts toward our parents. We are happy, and we've forgotten how to laugh. What a bunch of contradictions we are!

A healthy, vigorous, passionate life can be ours, but there are vast implications. The key to such a life is clear: each of us must love himself or herself. That unique person, that "I" who is precious to God, must be embraced in its entirety.

I

Why don't we instantly appropriate God's love and allow its power to work miracles within us?

I would venture to say that the most difficult job in the world is to know ourselves and deal with ourselves—and to accept all that it means to be human. Walker Percy, in his provocative, funny, and engaging book, *Lost in the Cosmos,* asks, "Why is it possible to learn more in ten minutes about the Crab Nebula in Taurus, which is 6,000 light years away, than you presently know about yourself, even though you've been stuck with yourself all your life?"[1]

We seem to be extraordinarily smart about everything except ourselves—as in that *New Yorker* cartoon where a rotund and obviously successful executive is talking to an equally successful colleague. He says, "I've really learned a lot over my sixty-three years. Unfortunately, almost all of it is about aluminum."

The implications of healthy, passionate life are vast and radical. We must love ourselves. It takes courage to embrace ourselves—the whole person—but that's where we must start.

Can you put your arms around yourself and say, "I love you?" Why not?

Thomas Merton once said, "What can we gain by sailing to the moon if we are not able to cross the abyss that separates us from ourselves?"

In my congregation a few years ago, I asked people to write me with suggestions for sermon topics. Many more than I would have expected asked, "How can I love myself if I have had so many failures?"

There is only one way. We must love ourselves because God does. And we must forgive ourselves because God does.

Yes, we must forgive ourselves for not being perfect. That's how we can begin to love ourselves. In a thousand and one different ways, all of us have made a mess out of our lives, and that makes us desperately lonely. We should be quick to admit that if we kicked the person who caused us most of our troubles, we couldn't sit down for a month!

Still, God wants all of us to come home to ourselves. It will be a great day when we do just that—when we meet ourselves and decide to come to terms with who we are. Yes, each of us is a bunch of contradictions. There are shadows and lights in us, demons and angels. But we *can* come home to ourselves. And it's life's most liberating moment when we put our arms around ourselves and become our own best friend. That is the person God knows through and through, and the person God loves forever.

II

I personally have had a fierce struggle in my journey toward self-acceptance and self-love.

There is a moment in Leonard Bernstein's modern opera, *Mass,* with which I identify in the most profound way. The priest celebrating the mass puts on one priestly vestment after another, one elegant robe on top of another. Then the priest staggers under the weight of all that tradition. There is a sense of violence in the scene, as if all that religiosity is about to destroy him. Finally the priest tears off all the vestments and stands in his blue jeans and a T-shirt before the altar. He sings, "Look at me. There is nothing but me under this."

It is a frightening scene, yet a reassuring one. For we see someone growing, someone becoming himself, someone willing to be human. And such vulnerability is always the crack in our armor through which the power of God enters our lives.

I know something about that scene. When I first became an ordained minister, I had so many battles going on inside of me. I refused to accept the darker side of my spirit. How could I be one commissioned by God to do God's holy work when there were so many weaknesses, so many conflicts, so much ugliness, so much darkness, so much confusion in my spirit?

So on with those vestments! I covered up and repressed that part of my life that was so threatening. But that was a costly thing to do. Denying part of myself created a fierce conflict within my spirit, and it also blocked the power of God that could have brought healing and transformation.

Only after a number of years, with the help of a compassionate psychoanalyst and the support of some strong friends who held me accountable but cared about me for what I was, was I able to put my arms around myself—all of me—and love the contradictions and conflicts and weaknesses as well as the wonders within me. But doing that led to the miracle of transformation, for radical self-acceptance always releases the divine energies that push us toward the destiny God has in store for us.

We don't have to be perfect for God to love us passionately. We don't have to repair ourselves to gain God's love. We don't have to put on a lot of paraphernalia to cover up the truth about ourselves in order to gain God's companionship.

The great Oliver Cromwell of England once sat for his portrait. The artist, in awe of this austere man, flattered him as he painted the portrait. When Cromwell saw the finished painting, he was furious. He shouted, "Paint me as I am, warts and all!" That is the way Jesus, our Savior, loves us, and we need to love ourselves in exactly the same way. Once we accept ourselves, we are on the path to wholeness.

I know it's still a difficult task. "I simply don't want to hug that dumb stuff that's inside me! I have no intention of putting my arms around me! I disgust myself!" So erupted a man to me on his way out of church one Sunday. But we will live stunted lives until we accept the fact that there is only one of each of us—with all the wonder and all the bleakness of the human spirit. And there is no power for life without a certain basic self-love.

Arthur Miller wrote his brilliant play, *After the Fall*, right after the suicide of Marilyn Monroe, who had been his wife. In writing the play, he was dealing with forgiving himself and others, and in it he put a haunting line that has stayed with me over the years: "One must finally take one's life into one's arms and kiss it."[2]

That is powerful. This acceptance releases power for growth in you.

The Color Purple is Alice Walker's prize-winning story and film of the suffering, endurance, and triumph of a black woman in the rural South. Celie is a poor, unlettered, unloved, "ugly" southern black girl. She is abused by her father and brutalized by her husband. But over the period of forty years which Alice Walker's story covers, we see the incredible transformation of Celie into a great woman. I think it all started when Shug kept saying to Celie, "You are something; you are something." Shug, the sometimes mistress of Celie's husband, cares deeply for Celie, and she wants her to see and know how unique and lovely she truly is. The moment in the movie that Celie begins to accept herself—and put her arms around herself—there comes across her face an incandescent smile I will never forget.

The remarkable Jewish writer, Elie Wiesel, tells this story in his book, *Souls on Fire*: When we die and we go to heaven, and we meet our maker, our maker is not going to say to us, why didn't you become a messiah? Why didn't you discover the cure for such-and-such? The only thing we're going to be asked at that precious moment is, why didn't you become you?

III

The consequences of our not loving ourselves are far-reaching.

We are created to be lovers of the human family and to put our arms around this broken world. The world's hope depends on that love. But none of us can truly love another person if we don't love ourselves. You can't give away what you don't have.

A child is doing her homework and asks her mom, "How did war begin?"

"Well, it was when Germany invaded Belgium," the mother replies.

The father interrupts, "That wasn't it."

Nettled by the intrusion, she retorts, "Sally did not ask you. She asked me."

"True, but tell her the facts."

"Why do you always interfere? Who asked you anyway?"

Husband and wife go at it hammer and tong. Finally, Sally says, "It's all right, Mom. I think I know how wars begin."

In a nation of increasing violence, where 67 percent of city dwellers are afraid to walk the streets at night and where one out of three is mugged or robbed in the course of a year; in a world of increasing terrorism and oppression, where conflicts are solved by violence and where courageous, unrelenting negotiation is becoming a lost art; in the world of our private landscapes, where there is also a great violence—tempers lashing out, children being abused, the weak being pushed around by the powerful, and everyone retaliating in harsh and subtle ways against those who hurt them—in that kind of world we long for peace.

But if there is to be peace among the nations, peace in our cities, peace within the families of the world—then we must have an internal disarmament, a truce to the internal civil war, a creative resolution to those inner conflicts. And that is no small task.

We long for peace. We commit ourselves to the priority of peacemaking. But the seeds of war are within us. We who are committing ourselves to the cause of ending the deadly arms race and bringing peace with justice to the earth's people— we should not forget the person within that we bring to this cause, for who would doubt that war is first made in the hearts of people?

A life that contributes to the world's peace awaits each of us. The key to such a life is clear: We must love ourselves. That's the heart of the matter.

God's steadfast, unconditional love surrounds us and seeks to enfold us. Yet God's power to transform us awaits our willingness to appropriate that divine love in the deep places of our lives.

One of the most neglected and misunderstood teachings of the Christian religion is the doctrine of justification by faith, made famous by Martin Luther. The term itself is heavy, and most explanations are usually heavier still. But what this term means is simply this: our loving acceptance by God isn't something we strive for, work for, or earn by good living. It is what God has already given us in Jesus. Faith is our acceptance in deep gratitude of God's acceptance of us just as we are.

God loves us as we are, "warts and all." As we come to accept that unpurchasable love, it becomes a powerful dynamism pushing us toward completion. If we do accept this wonderful, gracious gift of God's love, we won't stay the same, and we won't rest or be satisfied until we become what God created us to be. This theological statement is at the heart of the Christianity of the New Testament.

It is not possible to utter a hope more fundamental than the hope for peace. To allow hope to topple despair and cynicism in a world so starkly permeated by violence is a great victory. It is the victory of the spirit of God at work within us, pushing us toward the things that can create a peaceful world.

The first step toward creating a peace-filled world is for each of us to become who he or she is. That's our primary responsibility. And we can find the strength to do that when we accept the person that now lives inside and is loved by God.

IV

Once we have put our arms around ourselves, we can reach out and embrace this broken and divided world.

We can't give what we don't have. Each of us is something—wonderful, unique in all the world. The more we love ourselves, the more we have to give to others.

Most of our animosities against other people are hostilities which we feel against ourselves. If I am angry with myself, displeased and discontented with myself—then I am going to project that poor image of myself on other people.

Mark Twain said, "What a person sees in the human race is merely himself in the deep and honest privacy of his own heart."

If I have little value in my own eyes, if I am of little worth to myself, if I am filled with hostilities and conflicts, then I vent that fury towards myself by beating up the other fellow.

There is only one escape from that deadly scenario. I must accept myself, love myself, value myself as I am—"warts and all." Then there is liberation and energy to love the world.

That, I believe, is a central affirmation of authentic religion. God loves and accepts us as we are. If we accept that grace for ourselves, we can expect a miracle in human relationships. We will inevitably begin to treat people differently.

We start with "me," but we don't stop with "me." Those who love in the grace of divine love can broaden the "me" to "us." We can wondrously put our arms around ourselves—and then that releases in us the power of God for peace-filled, passionate, loving life for the world. Saying not "my world" but "our world" brings us to the divine power that can heal and redeem.

If each one of us could reach out today in love to another human being and accept that person as God has accepted us, we could change the world. The urgent imperative of the God who loves us with such steadfast, unconditional love is that we respond by embracing this violent, broken world with healing love.

Chapter Eleven

You Must Hug the
Planet Earth

In Morris West's gripping novel, *The Clowns of God,* a daughter is speaking to her father about going to Paris to live with her boyfriend. She wants to be with him now because she is afraid.

"Afraid of what?" the father asks.

"Of getting married and having children and trying to make a home, while the whole world could tumble round our ears in a day. You older ones don't understand. You've survived a war. You've built things. . . . You've had us; we're grown up. But look at the world you've left us! All along the borders there are rocket launchers and missile silos. . . . You've given us everything except tomorrow. I don't want my baby to be born in a bomb shelter and die of radiation sickness!"[1]

I am deeply concerned that my generation may have given youth everything except tomorrow. I want to change that. Some words of Lillian Hellman about the arms race have grasped my heart: "It no longer matters whose fault it is. It matters that this game be stopped. We want to declare that there are still men and women in the world who do not think it is dangerous or radical to declare themselves for the continuation of life."

We need a new sense of purpose if this planet is to have a future. Radical evaluations are needed if we are to count for breaking the cycle of violence and bringing peace to the earth.

And radical change is possible, as vividly illustrated by the story of Alfred Nobel, the inventor of dynamite who amassed a fortune by selling the weapons of destruction. One morning in 1888, Nobel was quite surprised to read his own obituary in a French newspaper. Obviously, it was a journalistic mistake.

One of his brothers had died, and a careless reporter had used a prewritten obituary of the wrong man.

But as he read, Nobel was shocked and deeply disturbed to learn what the world really thought about him. He was seen simply as the dynamite king, the merchant of death, who had made a great fortune out of explosives. Nobel had hoped his inventions would be useful to people and to nations; yet he was viewed as one who dealt in blood and war for profit.

At that moment, Alfred Nobel resolved to show the world the true purpose of his life. He revised his will so that his fortune would be dedicated to the recognition of great creative achievements—with the highest award going to those who had done the most for world peace. From then on Nobel's image began to change. Now, a century later, we remember him the way he wanted us to.

I am concerned that we in the Christian community find a way to place ourselves with those who are working for a world freed of nuclear terror—and also find a way to engage ourselves in the struggle to create that world where we can live in decency and peace.

In the last chapter I described the internal dimensions of peace. If there is to be peace among nations, peace in our cities, peace in our families, then we must have an internal disarmament, a truce to the internal civil war, a creative resolution to those internal conflicts. If there is to be any hope that we can possibly reach across the Pacific Ocean in love and affirm those in other countries as friends and brothers and sisters, we must first deal lovingly and creatively with ourselves.

But peace also has an external dimension. We must take hold of this, too, and root it down in those deep places if we are to be faithful to the Christian imperative of peacemaking. I believe this, too, has a vast and critical implication for anyone who seeks a healthy and passionate life.

As I have studied the New Testament over the years, I have grown increasingly convinced that the Christian church must be a community of peacemakers. And this has many implications. But in my mind it definitely involves protesting the misuse of military power to settle political problems and overcoming the widespread blindness to the social despair that makes for revolution.

Christian churches can't stick to safe and manageable subjects as the world convulses in violence. The Christian church must stop blessing war and must become a resistance movement. The followers of Jesus are to be peace's strongest advocates.

I am keenly aware of how many people want a church which will give them comfort and lift burdens from their hearts. Life can be hard and cruel, and we come to a church seeking relief; we come seeking a God who can bind up our broken hearts.

That desire is very legitimate. But in the midst of that deep desire, I place the words of Jesus: "Whoever cares for his own safety is lost; but if a man will let himself be lost for my sake, he will find his true self" (Matt. 16:25). The biblical truth seems beyond dispute: Our participation in meeting the needs of our brothers and sisters of the world is an absolute prerequisite to our gaining life's deepest meaning. Only as we lose ourselves in love for the human family will we find that divine love that will never let us go. We bear a burden and find joy. We soothe another's wounds and are healed.

A church that helps people in their search for passionate living will hold these two dimensions—internal and external peace—inextricably together.

There are some theological and ethical considerations in responding to the imperative of peacemaking.

I

The basic theological presupposition which undergirds my profound concern about the escalating nuclear arms race is that this is God's world and faithful stewards will preserve it.

To whom does the earth belong? That is the primary question for those who claim to live in the Hebrew-Christian tradition.

To whom does the earth belong? Not to George Regas or the Episcopal Church, not to the President or the Secretary of State, not to the United States or the Soviet Union, not to the universities, the banks, the corporations. The earth belongs to God, and you and I are here because we've been given the precious gift of life by the Creator. The psalmists proclaim it over and over again: "The earth is the Lord's and all that is in it, the world and those who dwell therein. For it was he who founded it upon the seas and planted it firm upon the waters beneath" (Ps. 24:1–2); "Know that the Lord is God; he has made us and we are his own, his people, the flock which he shepherds. Enter his gates with thanksgiving and his courts with praise" (100:3–4). That affirmation is at the very core of a biblical religion. And a primary obligation of a person of conscience is to be a faithful steward and preserve the creation.

It is nearly impossible to overstate the perilous danger we have created through the nuclear arms race. We are told by our scientists that the universe has been in existence for twenty billion years. The solar system has existed for six billion years—the earth for almost five billion years; something resembling human life for three million years. And civilization as we know it is estimated to be ten thousand years old. But the last forty years—the nuclear age—have brought us to the brink of annihilation.

We are quite literally thirty minutes away from the end of civilization as we know it. It takes only thirty minutes for a missile launched by either the Soviet Union or the United States to reach its target. Thirty minutes from the end!

There have been a hundred generations since Moses said to the people, "I hold before you life and death; therefore choose life" (Deut. 30:19). But we are the first generation that by choosing death could destroy the planet.

"God saw all that he had made, and it was very good" (Gen. 1:31). I believe the basic, pivotal, fundamental, ethical duty of our age is keeping the planet together and saving the human family.

II

I also believe our nuclear policies and the escalating arms race come under the judgment of God.

If we keep our nuclear policies at arm's length from our religious convictions, we can do what is wrong and call it right. We must bring it all into the light of Jesus and the broad sweep of the biblical tradition.

The prophecy of Zechariah was that Jesus, full of compassion, would be like the morning sun from heaven that would rise before us, "to shine on those who live in darkness, under the cloud of death, and to guide our feet into the way of peace" (Luke 1:78–79).

I am quite aware that there is more than one side for religious people to be on in the peace question. And I know I need to be wary about too pretentiously accepting the mantle of prophecy and claiming God's will for my position. I am cautioned by that seventeenth century quotation from an anonymous author: "I would rather see coming at me a whole battalion with drawn swords than one lone Calvinist convinced he is doing the will of God." And yet I believe with all my heart that a careful, ethical consideration of the arms race would say we are going in the wrong direction.

In my view, we have allowed this nation to place its security in nuclear weapons which are militarily unusable, morally outrageous, and economically disastrous. In the light of Christ's life and witness, that is the ultimate insanity of our day.

War has always been tragic; it has now become preposterous. But before any final ethical judgment is made about nuclear weapons and policies, we must get into our heads and hearts the reality of our peril. We've built ourselves into an era of nuclear absurdity. One miscalculation and the human family is vaporized.

The one atom bomb dropped on Hiroshima killed 130,000 people in a city of 340,000. In a space of seconds the city was turned into hell. But that terrible moment more than forty years ago pales in comparison to what a nuclear holocaust would mean today. Together the United States and the Soviet Union have 50,000 nuclear weapons, and at present each side is making three nuclear bombs every day. The world's stockpile of nuclear weapons is the equivalent of 1.5 million bombs of the destructive power of Hiroshima. That stunning fact creates the quintessential moral issue of our age.

It is within this context of destructive power that influential, respected people in the United States speak of fighting a nuclear war, surviving, and even winning it! Those at high levels of government service—presidents included—have fueled such talk.

Nuclear weapons are usable and the war is winnable—in my mind that's the talk of madness, the talk of sin, the talk of a dead conscience. Dr. Marvin Goldberger, president of the prestigious California Institute of Technology in Pasadena, has said in my presence that anyone who talks of winning a nuclear war is certifiably insane. That is not the hyperbole of an iconoclastic preacher, but the words of one of America's most distinguished atomic scientists.

Even among those policymakers wise enough to know a nuclear war is not winnable, there is still the commitment to the policy of nuclear deterrence. What does that mean?

We must keep clear in our minds that at the heart of all the discussion about nuclear weapons and the policies of nuclear deterrence is the reality that the United States and the Soviet Union are ready, under certain circumstances, to commit mass slaughter on an unprecedented scale. Nuclear deterrence means we are willing at some point to rain thermonuclear weapons down on our adversaries and make victims of the innocent—babies and women and elderly people. And the Soviet Union is poised with the same intention. A recent study out of the United Nations contends that an all-out nuclear war with its effect of nuclear winter will kill four billion people.

I believe God judges those policies and plans. And plans that make a nuclear holocaust possible are rendered immoral by every test of the Christian tradition. Christian ethics

would call such an act a crime against God and humanity.
The New Testament is uncompromising: "If a man says, 'I
love God', while hating his brother, he is a liar" (1 John 4:19).
The Bible makes it unmistakably clear that in the person who
follows God there is no place for hatred. "Everyone who loves
is a child of God and knows God, but the unloving know
nothing of God" (1 John 4:8).

What does it say about the moral values of a nation that it
is willing to use genocidal weapons against the enemy and
commit suicide in the process? What does it say about a
Christian church that it does not place its very life against
such a national policy? Shortly after the development of the
nuclear bomb, the great ethicist, Reinhold Niebuhr, stated
that an enemy's using these weapons against us would mean
our physical annihilation; but our using them against an enemy would mean our moral annihilation.

It is no wonder then that for over forty years of experience
with nuclear weapons the great majority of people have pre-
ferred not to think about the matter at all and have left it to
the experts.

I think religious communities have played an important
role over the last few years in making the nuclear arms issue
central to the American political scene. The issue of nuclear
war has been taken from the back shelves of the mind, where
most people have put it for so long, and has been placed
forcefully upon the conscience. More and more, a conscience
shaped by the Spirit of Jesus and by the Old Testament
prophets is saying no to nuclear war.

Several years ago, during a debate on nuclear policy, Dr.
Adda Boseman, a well-known political science professor at
Sarah Lawrence College, said something to me that still rings
in my ears: "Churches go too far if they try to instruct political leaders on the immorality of nuclear war. . . . Nuclear
war is not the worst thing," she said. "The loss of liberty and
loss of country are worse."

We prize our freedom. We love our country. But we who
live in the Christian community must say it clearly: Nuclear
war is immoral. We cannot choose the way of Christ and also

hold a willingness to engage in the destruction of the human race. The Christian community must say it decisively: It is better to lose everything we have than to lose everything we are.

III

The solidarity of the human race gives perspective to our ethical considerations of nuclear war.

On this spaceship Earth we all ride together—Soviets, Americans, Chinese, Lebanese, Salvadorans, Cubans, French, Nicaraguans—all four and a half billion of us are riders together. We have a common mission, and that is to preserve this precious planet Earth and live together in the great, wonderful human family.

Sir Fred Hoyle in 1948 said, "Once a photograph of the earth taken from outside is available—a new idea as powerful as any in history will be let loose." Now such photographs are available, and they show clearly that it's one world. There are no boundaries; we are interconnected. The survival of one is dependent on the survival of all. As the apostle Paul puts it, "We are members one of another" (Eph. 4:25, RSV). In the nuclear age, the smallest unit of survival is the whole world.

William Sloane Coffin puts it in a way that adds a different dimension to our understanding: "In that solidarity with the Russians we need to see that if we are not bound together by our love—we are certainly bound together by our sins."

I have many disagreements with the "Moral Majority," and the "Religious Right," but chief among them is that they preach something that to me is clearly theologically and psychologically unhealthy. They seem to say that evil is "out there;" evil is in the other person. Evil is not in me, but in you, to be fought and defeated. Goodness is in us and our cause.

Those preachers should know the Bible better than that. The Bible speaks of an overwhelming sense of good and evil in all of life. *The dividing line of good and evil slices through every heart.* Paul put it this way: "The good which I want to do, I fail to do; but what I do is the wrong which is against my will" (Rom. 7:19).

If we are to make our way to peace, we must take the high road away from self-righteousness. St. Augustine said it sixteen hundred years ago: "Never fight evil as if it were something that arose totally outside yourself."

We should not be blind to the terrible things the Soviet Union has done and is doing. Much of their system of government and much of their international behavior are repugnant to me. There has been a vicious cruelty at work in that government. Their brutal invasion of Afghanistan and their sustaining that deadly conflict is rightly condemned. And their inability to admit to any of their horrible mistakes is a very disturbing phenomenon.

But the United States is not without its own terrible sins. We, too, have had difficulty owning up to some of our treacherous deeds. The cost of the carnage in the Vietnam war was staggering. Yet President Reagan is still contending we should have declared war and finished the job. For, as the President said in a press conference on April 4, 1984, "Maybe General MacArthur was right, 'There is no substitute for victory.'" In numerous trips to Nicaragua, I have seen with my own eyes and felt with my own heart the great human tragedies that have come out of our government's support of the Contras.

The Soviets and Americans are riders together on this spaceship Earth, and we are bound together by our sins. An acceptance of that fact would move us closer to peace.

At this writing, the United States and the Soviet Union have had several summit meetings—some successful and some less so. But hopefully there will be another between Ronald Reagan and Mikhail Gorbachev—or whoever are the American and Soviet leaders of the day. And I have a fantasy—and a deep hope—of how that meeting between the leaders of the two greatest powers on earth will go. Gorbachev begins, "Mr. President, you have no idea of the terrible things we Russians have done over the years." The President interrupts, "Please, Mikhail, you haven't a clue to all the horrible things we have done at home and abroad." That would be the high road away from self-righteousness, toward an honest acceptance that we are bound together in our sins.

We are bound together in a world community. And there is good and evil, beauty and ugliness, greatness and shame, truth and falsehood, in us all! If we can acknowledge that and move away from self-righteousness, then we will unleash the greatest healing power the world has ever known. Then we could no longer demonize the Russians, picturing our values as the antithesis of theirs—our honesty and their deceit, our freedom and their slavery, our peaceful institutions and their warlike militarism.

If we Americans and Russians are not brothers and sisters bound together by our love, then at least we are bound by our sins.

IV

The three theological considerations I have mentioned— that this is God's world and we are its stewards, that nuclear policies come under God's judgment, that we in the world are all bound together on spaceship Earth—push me in certain directions of action in behalf of this precious planet and her people.

First, I seek to do everything I can to influence a reversal of the nuclear arms race and a radical reduction of our nuclear arsenal in cooperation with and in struggle with the Soviet Union.

And I am not alone in this conviction. The proposed direction toward arms build-up is officially declared immoral by many major Christian denominations. Statements by the Episcopal Church and the American Roman Catholic Bishops in 1982 and 1983 on the morality of nuclear deterrence are unambiguously clear: The only way nuclear deterrence can be considered moral at all is that it provides the umbrella under which significant nuclear arms control progress can be made and radical reductions in weapons achieved in the world's nuclear arsenals. Without this movement, nuclear deterrents are rendered immoral. The Methodist Bishops in 1986 said the policy of nuclear deterrence cannot receive the Church's blessing under any circumstances.

I believe we must stop the arms race. I believe the very soul of the Christian church rests on our efforts. In my opinion, the clearest way to do that is to work for the passage of a comprehensive test ban treaty by the United States and the Soviet Union, for if a country doesn't test, it can't develop new weapons.

I still believe our American democracy works well enough that the priorities and values in people's minds do get translated into national policy. If enough people want to end the escalating arms race, it will happen. Congress could cut off funds for nuclear testing if we made it clear that this was the moral passion of the American people. That, I believe, would be a godly act. It would bring us closer to peace and the preservation of planet Earth.

A second action grows out of these theological considerations. I am committed to work for peace with justice. Justice must be central to all our efforts for peace. That is the true meaning of the biblical word *shalom.*

The story is told of a baseball game between the Los Angeles Dodgers and the San Diego Padres. It was the ninth inning, the score was tied, and the bases were loaded. The pitcher stepped off the mound, picked up some resin, and then made the sign of the cross. The batter thereupon stepped out of the batter's box, knocked the dirt from his spikes, and also made the sign of the cross. The umpire behind the home plate coughed a bit and was then overheard to pray, "O Lord, please don't take sides. Just watch the game."

One thing you can count on for sure. In this game of life, God has definitely taken sides. But I am not talking about East or West, the U.S. or Russia, liberal or conservative. God is definitely pro peace, pro compassion, pro love, pro justice.

God's concern for the orphans, the widows, the strangers runs like a refrain through the Old Testament. They represent the casualties of life, the powerless and the voiceless in the system, those broken by injustice and apathy.

This compassionate concern for the poor is a constant theme of the Psalms: "You ought to give judgment for the weak and the orphan, and see right done to the destitute and downtrodden, you ought to rescue the weak and the poor, and save them from the clutches of wicked men" (Ps. 82:3–4). "Happy the man who has a concern for the helpless!" (41:1).

The prophets are stern in proclaiming God's judgment upon those who neglect the poor. Isaiah speaks: "Shame on you! you who make unjust laws and publish burdensome decrees, depriving the poor of justice, robbing the weakest of my people of their rights, despoiling the widow and plundering the orphan" (Isa. 10:1–2). "Is not this what I require of you as a fast: to loose the fetters of injustice, to untie the knots of the yoke, to snap every yoke and set free those who have been crushed? . . . Then shall your light break forth like the dawn and soon you will grow healthy like a wound newly healed" (58:6, 8).

Amos even says that the divine love for the poor is so great that God will shut God's ears to our prayers if we neglect the needy: "I will not delight in your sacred ceremonies. When you present your sacrifices and offerings I will not accept them. . . . Spare me the sound of your songs; I cannot endure the music of your lutes. Let justice roll on like a river and righteousness like an ever-flowing stream" (Amos 5:21–24).

In Jesus' parable of the rich man who lives in great magnificence while he is oblivious to Lazarus, the desperately poor man who begs by the city gate, those themes of the Old Testament find a blazing focus (Luke 16:19–31). Jesus unsparingly condemns irresponsibility, our lack of compassionate concern in personal and national life.

So what practical steps can we take to work for peace with justice as the Bible so clearly calls us to do? One way is to do all we can to see that the Federal budget gives priority to justice for the poor. If you want peace, work for justice. And for a disciple of Jesus, the arms race is a gross distortion of just priorities in our nation.

People are sick and hungry all over the planet, and the world is spending $900 billion a year on arms. To my mind, that ordering of priorities is madness. I don't believe the followers of Jesus want that. Pope Paul VI said the arms race is a criminal mismanagement of humanity's resources. President Eisenhower said, "Every gun that's made, every plane constructed, every bomb manufactured, signifies, in the final sense, a theft from those who are hungry and not fed, those who are cold and not clothed."

I believe the followers of Jesus must stand for life over and against death. Let these facts about God's human family go into the deep places of our conscience:

- $900 billion a year on arms—and 1.5 billion of God's precious people go without professional health care;
- $900 billion on arms—and 1 billion precious people live in absolute poverty and constant malnutrition;
- $900 billion on arms—and 650 million school-age children of the world have never been to school;
- $900 billion on arms—and the gap between the rich and poor nations has doubled since 1960;
- $900 billion on arms, which is $2 billion per day—and in Africa 14,000 children die of hunger and hunger-related diseases each day; and four days of military spending would end starvation in the world; and 12 hours of military spending would eradicate malaria in the world;
- $900 billion on arms—and here in America, the richest nation in the world, there are 35 million who live in poverty; and the Federal budget has slashed programs for the poor and the sick and the unemployed and the children as it increases the money available for military programs. Now "Star Wars," taking weapons into space, is being sought by both Democrats and Republicans. The cost of "Star Wars" to the taxpayers is staggering. For research alone over five years the cost has been estimated to be between $500 billion and $1 trillion. And through it all the poor are asked to carry the highest cost for this competitive arms race. When the financial belt is tightened, it is always around the necks of the poor. I believe this is scandalous. We must put the words of the Bible in the center of our conscience: "If a man has enough to live

on, and yet when he sees his brother in need shuts up his heart against him, how can it be said that the divine love dwells in him?" (1 John 3:17).

I am glad the President and Nancy Reagan are pushing us toward a drug-free culture. I join them in that campaign. I am distressed, however, at the paucity of funds available. We now spend around $2 billion a year on drug and alcohol abuse. $1.8 billion of this goes to law enforcement. This is good. We need it, and it is double what it was five years ago. But we spent $200 million on all the rest—education, treatment, research. The treatment money for drug addicts has been reduced by 40 percent since 1982. The waiting time for drug treatment clinics in Los Angeles is four to six months. I believe this is scandalous.

National security means more than military power. It also means a just social order. It means healthy and well-educated children. It means a nation of beautiful cities and vigorous economies. Both Republicans and Democrats alike have allowed militarism to be the predominant force in American life.

Without a shot being fired, the arms race is killing people. As I have struggled with these hard issues over the years, I believe in the deep places of my own Christ-formed conscience that God wants me to act. I believe God is urgently calling Christian churches to place their lives against those grossly distorted priorities.

V

Hold on to hope if you truly want to make your life count for peace among nations.

On September 1, 1983, a South Korean commercial airliner veered off course en route from Anchorage to Seoul and flew over the Sakhalin Islands, a highly sensitive military area for the Soviet Union. After the Soviets had tracked the Boeing 747 jumbo airliner for two and a half hours, a Soviet pilot followed the orders of his military commander and fired two missiles. The plane was hit and tumbled out of the sky, plummeting thirty-two thousand feet into the Sea of Japan. Two hundred sixty-nine men, women and children were killed. Whether the Soviet military command knew it was a commercial airliner is still not known. But minutes before it was about to leave the Soviet territory, it was blown out of the sky. And with that horrible massacre of almost three hundred people on Flight 007, so many hopes and dreams for peace on earth were shattered.

A friend of mine, who has helped us in our work at All Saints Church to reverse the arms race, was despairing when he talked with me about that tragic event. "The Soviets ruined everything. That blunder has rallied support for the MX, new missiles in Europe, and more dollars for defense. When that missile shot down the Korean airliner, it shot down my hopes for arms control," my friend sadly commented.

We who are followers of the Prince of Peace, we who have committed ourselves to be peace's strongest advocates, do not have the luxury of such despair. I share Harvey Cox's conviction that "our greatest enemy is not, certainly not, the Russians . . . or even the Pentagon. Our greatest enemy is our fatalism, our resignation."

Hold on to hope—it is your greatest gift to the world. In the words of scientist and theologian Pierre Teilhard de Chardin: "The world of tomorrow belongs to those who brought it its greatest hope."

We are messengers of hope, especially to children. No gift to a child can compare to the hope that we have not given up on the future.

A teacher asked her class of fifth graders what they thought the possibilities were that we would experience a nuclear war. Most of the children were convinced such a war would come about, with the exception of one little girl who was determined that this would not be the case. When the teacher asked her why she felt so strongly that nuclear war would not occur, she replied, "Because my daddy and mommy are working all the time to make sure it doesn't happen." The darkest of nights will not put out our hope if we have a few parents like that.

There are so many forces at work moving this world toward

its destruction. Yet people who love God and God's precious creation are called to hold on to hope. And our task as a people of hope? To keep life's incredible possibilities before an individual and a church and a city and a nation; to keep saying to a world apparently condemned to destruction, "You can live"; to say it is possible to feed the hungry, to free the world from racial and sexual and religious prejudices, and to end war forever.

Hope is one of those paradoxes of Christian life: We must live as if the future of all creation depended on us, while at the same time we live secure in the belief that God's love and power is supreme—and such a trust makes us hopeful in the darkest hour.

One of those dark times for me was the assassination of Senator Robert Kennedy in 1968. It was the third assassination of a national leader in five years—first President John Kennedy, then Martin Luther King, Jr., and now this. It was a dismal, tragic time in the life of America. My eyes were fixed on the television, watching the funeral mass from St. Patrick's Cathedral in New York, trying to assimilate the shock and grief of the assassination of another great public servant.

At the conclusion of the service, the casket was carried out of St. Patrick's as the choir sang Handel's Hallelujah Chorus: "Hallelujah, for the Lord God omnipotent reigneth . . . King of Kings and Lord of Lords. Hallelujah!" Never have I heard it more majestic and beautiful. There in that burning focus, that flashing, painful moment, was the entire history of the world. Guns and hatred and death—yet God. Blood and smoke and suffering—yet that song which began at a stable in Bethlehem and ended with a tomb in Jerusalem. "Hallelujah! The Lord God omnipotent reigneth." It was the proclamation of the ultimate victory of God—and the victory of justice and peace and love.

"The Lord our God, sovereign over all, has entered on his reign! Exult and shout for joy" (Rev. 19:6). This defiant hope during the worst of times does not allow us to sit back in the face of evil. It is not a reinforcement of the attitude, "Let God do it; there isn't one thing we can do about it." Rather, our defiant hope releases in us the energy to go to work and preserve the precious creation God has entrusted to us. Anything else would be sinful disobedience.

It is said that what Satan missed the most when he fell from heaven were the trumpets in the morning. From the darkest of nights will come God's daybreak. As we struggle for a new world at a time when the clock is so close to midnight, we hear those trumpets and live in the wildest hope that God rules creation and will ultimately bring life out of death.

In this deep trust we go about the work of peacemaking. This work will lead us to do things we never imagined we could do, and in that process we will become the people God created us to be. Our lives will have the joy that comes from knowing that what we do really matters.

We follow the way of peace secure in the promise that the Holy Spirit will sustain us, no matter how difficult the task, no matter how long it takes. God will lead us, empower us, and never abandon us. God gives us such a hope. And the darkest of nights will not destroy it.

Part Five

Resources for the Journey

Chapter Twelve

Perseverance: Standing Firm and Gaining Life

I can still picture him in my mind. He sat slumped in my office and shared with me how totally defeated he felt. "I am so tired of life, so exhausted at not being able to get anywhere, so discouraged. My job seems beyond my capabilities; my family isn't in a good place; my wife hasn't a clue about what is going on inside of me. It's all so hard and complex. But worst of all, I fear that I am not going to be able to hold on much longer."

Maybe you've been right there with this man. I know I have. Life is hard, and its difficulties are so everlastingly daily! It gets into your bones after a while. We all get tired—physically, spiritually, mentally. Dr. Paul Dudley White, the famous heart specialist in Boston, used to say that the most common complaint he heard in his medical practice was, "I'm tired."

Life isn't easy; it seems like trouble is on every side. A woman told me the most characteristic expression of her sixteen-year old son is a sigh. He gets up sighing and he goes to bed sighing!

We can all understand that. Life is hard, full of crises, and we feel powerless to change it. We are not in control. Yet deep within us is the stirring to live life passionately, completely; something deep within keeps pushing us toward wholeness and beauty. We still believe in those flowers growing out of a rock crevice; we still recognize that difficulties are opportunities for growth, that failure is an open door to the future, that "the iron box of frustration contains treasures of insight and strength"—to use Robert Raines' words.[1]

Count Leo Tolstoy once described four ways people face

disappointment and hardship, four ways they handle their
humanness:
- Frightened, they go out and get drunk.
- They give way to despair and refuse to deal with life.
- They resent it and harden their hearts to it and to the
  world.
- There are some who accept it, stand up to it, and courageously transform it into a richness by a union with the
  divine resources of the universe.

I know which option I aspire to! The question is how to do it.
The issue is not so much to find an explanation for what is
happening to us. There are mysteries we can never solve. But
we *can* endure, and we can grow. I love what Miguel de Unamuno, in the *Tragic Sense of Life*, says: "The end of life is not
understanding but living."

We don't want to be defeated by life. We want success. But
nine times out of ten the reason we are defeated, the reason
we lie down on life instead of standing up to it, is that we just
run out of power. What breaks us down is an external strain
plus a sense of internal inadequacy to meet it.

And so we seek adequate resources for the journey. Deep
within us, I believe, something seeks to be connected with the
divine energy that replaces discouragement with hope and
apathy with courage and weakness with strength. We want a
union with the resurrection power.

There are ways to link ourselves to those resources that
make us adequate for the hard, exciting, challenging, wonderful journey. Let's look at two.

I

We make a decision never to give up, and that decision
releases the divine energies that empower us to finish the
race.

We live in a culture where escapism is a way of life. Fleeing
the hard tasks of life, going from place to place, job to job,
person to person, seeking satisfaction and ease—I believe this
is the new hedonism of our time. The dominant wisdom seems

to be that in this nuclear age there may be no tomorrow—so we might as well enjoy the pleasures of the moment. That escapism takes so many forms: drugs, alcohol, frantic overwork, promiscuous sexual activity, or a personal fantasyland. But most of us are on the run one way or the other. Somewhere deep within us is the desperate hope that if we plunge into enough activities, whatever is wrong out there will somehow go away.

There is a cartoon which depicts a motorist halfway underneath his station wagon, trying to fix it while a broiling sun beats down overhead. His children are peering out the rear window and offering their father advice. The caption has the exasperated father responding to his restless children, "But we can't switch channels. This isn't television, this is real!"

Escapism, in all its corroding forms, has become the moral atmosphere we breathe. There has grown up in our time an almost pathological desire to escape from the difficulties and responsibilities and drudgeries and even the realities of life.

All of us are on the run in some degree. Every one of us who has been tempted to quit, to run out on life, should know he or she is in good company. We all belong to the human race.

There is something deep in us that wants to respond to those words of Psalm 55: "Oh that I had the wings of a dove to fly away and be at rest" (v. 6). Don't we long to get away when life harasses us and we are pressed on every side? I often sigh with the psalmist—"Oh, for those wings to get away from it all." Who hasn't desired that—a change of scenery, a new job, a new town, a new moment conflict-free, a restful spot in the storm, a new start in life?

Don't misread me. Some measure of escape from life's strains is essential. In fact, getting away from the hectic pace for a weekend or escaping for a few weeks from the year's demanding intensity can actually keep us going when we are tempted to quit. (One of my favorite forms of relaxation amid the weekly pressures of my job is to escape from the realities of my life and bury myself in a B-grade movie, where I know life is going to work out successfully!)

Nevertheless, we must all face up to the facts. To live always on the wings of that dove, always in escape, fleeing the

hard tasks, going from place to place, from person to person,
seeking satisfaction and ease—that is a very corroding and
destructive process in our culture.

I acknowledge that even the strongest, most courageous
people have times of despair and exhaustion when they
would like those wings of a dove to fly away and rest. But the
doctors of the human spirit make it very clear that escapism
as a way of life is futile and debilitating to the inner life.

Those wings never carry us to a restful place; this age of
anxiety should tell us that. And the reason, I think, is clear.
Our escapism is a flight from reality, an attempt to get away
from ourselves—and that never works. D. H. Lawrence has
one of his characters saying, "Poor Richard Lovate wearies
himself to death struggling with the problem of himself—
while all the time calling it Australia." We will be who we are
wherever we go. Fleeing doesn't solve the problem, for we
always take ourselves with us.

I am haunted by a dreadful passage of Thomas Carlyle's in
which he pictured a man trying to escape from a veiled figure
who relentlessly pursued him. Every time he turned, it was
there—that black thing dogging him on and on. He would run
wildly, trying to escape, but it was still there. One day, franti-
cally, he seized the monster, tore away the veil, and was
stunned. The menacing thing was himself, the shadow cast by
his own image.

It is against that backdrop of a fleeing figure, living by
evasion and finding no rest or passionate vitality, that I want
the Bible to have its say.

St. Paul, a man who himself had fallen and had many failures scarring his life, still believed fiercely in the possibilities
of beginning again and pressing toward the goals of Christian
life. He wrote to the Philippians, "Stand . . . firm in the
Lord, my beloved" (Phil. 4:1).

And against a backdrop of weary people—tired of life, exhausted and discouraged by life's perplexities—we have these
words of Jesus: "By standing firm you will win true life for
yourselves" (Luke 21:19).

I believe the Spirit of God is urging this word upon our

hearts today: Stand firm! Stand up to life; don't run out—
and you will gain true life, beautiful, vital, passionate life for
yourself. That's a powerful picture to hang in the front room
of your mind—a person standing up to life, staying with it
when the going is fierce, deciding that whatever else might
happen, she just could not see herself running out on life.

Paul Scherer, the theologian, once said, "All great living
begins in the simple estimate we have of ourselves that will
not let us play the coward's role." One of the strongest de-
fenses our lives have is the self-respect that insists that because we are who we are—God's people—we draw the line
and say, "I won't run out on life."

Over the last few years I have discovered a strategy that
has become very health-giving to my life. I say to myself, "I
give up the right to quit." I make a permanent choice and
settle it once and for all that quitting on life is unthinkable.
And I find that when I make that decision to hold on, divine
energy is released into my life.

Life is not a short sprint; it is a marathon race. The rewards
of deep fulfillment in the Christian journey always come to
the long-distance runners. So the Bible says that if we hold
on till the end, we will gain life that is true and rich and deep
and fulfilling.

There is a story of a famous man who refused to have his
biography written in the days of his fame and when he was
alive. "I've seen too many people fall out on the last lap of the
race," he said.

"Stand firm to the end." The Spirit of God is saying to us in
those words that life isn't really safe till we reach our journey's end.

John Bunyan, in his dream, saw that from the very gate of
heaven there was a way to hell. And there is an ancient story
of an Italian painter which makes the point even more vividly.

This painter had been commissioned to portray the Last
Supper, so he scoured his entire neighborhood for appropriate models. He soon uncovered a ruddy, burly sort of fellow
with white flowing hair and had him sit for Peter. Next he ran
across an ascetic youth with brooding mouth and questioning

eyes, and chose him for Doubting Thomas. An eager, aggressive type of man became Andrew, and a youth with features of sensitive compassion and deep courage was picked to sit for Christ.

Before the month was out the painter had secured models for all twelve of the apostles except one. No matter how diligently he searched, he could not find a model suitable for the part of the betraying Judas Iscariot. So an important part of the canvas had to remain unfinished. Without the impact of the treacherous Judas, the Last Supper lost much of its meaning.

However, the artist never gave up his search. Wherever he went and whatever he did, he was always unconsciously on the lookout for a replica of the man who sold his Lord for thirty pieces of silver. At last, several years later, he finally found his Judas. There, slouched at a table in a cheap cafe, sat a sullen man in an alcoholic stupor. His face was ravaged by obvious self-indulgence. His eyes could not hide a troubled conscience which smoldered behind them. And his mouth was tense and cynical. He might almost have been Judas in the flesh.

Unimpressed by the opportunity of becoming a living part of the Last Supper, the hardened fellow sneered his refusal to cooperate. But the persistent artist finally won him over by appealing to the one love which still had any lure for him. He was promised a bag of gold whose worth was far beyond the usual model's fee.

During the last sitting, just as the painter was applying those finishing touches which would bring the canvas to its magnificent completion, the Judas model amazed him by suddenly bursting into tears.

"You don't know me, do you?"

"No, I don't. I only met you a few weeks ago."

"You never saw me before you picked me up that day in the cafe?"

"No, at least not to my knowledge."

"I am the man who once sat for your Christ in the painting!"

A good beginning and a sad ending is one of life's great

tragedies. "Anyone can write a good first act," Arnold Bennett used to say, "but how's your second act?" That calls for standing firm in the Lord, for perseverance, endurance, steadfastness, tenacity.

I've always felt we underestimate the incredible potential of sheer willpower, of exercising the determination to "stand firm in the Lord." How many of us are like the patient who went to see a doctor about a special problem. "Doctor," he said, "I want you to tell me how I can cure my tendency to lie in bed too long in the mornings." "Yes, I will," she responded. "I advise you to pull one leg over the bed and draw the other leg after it!"

Too often, I think, we go looking for spiritual exercises when God is telling us to go to work and use our brains and our willpower. When we do, God releases divine power for the journey.

Perseverance is a doorway into the storehouse of divine power. Whether it is a struggle for health, for a marriage, for a business, for faith and character, for a decent and just and peaceful world, quitting seldom makes sense.

I would add one cautious footnote to that, however; I do not mean to make absolutes out of perseverance and permanence. There are places in life, spaces in our experiences, which are destructive and even deadly. It is wise to accept the fact that there are times when we struggle and fail, and times when it is a beautiful act of grace to let go of that failure and move on. There are times when that is the only thing we can do with integrity. However, I am certain that moment when we should move on does not occur as often as our escapist culture would have us believe.

Come back to the words of Jesus: "By standing firm you will win true life for yourselves." He lived those words to the fullest measure.

Then, at the end of his life, with darkness all around, Jesus whispered, "It is finished" (John 19:30).

What a glorious thing to say at the end of the journey. "It is finished." I've accomplished the mission. I stayed the course. I fulfilled the new covenant—and against incredible odds.

That's what Jesus meant by those memorable words from the cross.

He had made his way through Palestine with God's commission to reach the lost and give them hope, to offer compassion and healing to a broken world, to lay bare for all to see the loving heart of God. He had gone to Jerusalem to challenge all the powers of evil with God's truth and to confront the hatred, corruption, and rigidity of many people in Jerusalem with God's inclusive love. The rejection of this love—the vituperations, the brutalities, the insults, the disappointments, the pain that crushed down upon him at the end had not turned his love sour or caused him to retaliate. Although deserted by his disciples, he had pressed on with that mission to the very end. And when it meant a humiliating death on a cross to say how deep and broad and wide were the mercies of God, Jesus had stumbled his way to Calvary.

"It is finished," Jesus whispered on the cross. In today's society full of people who quit when life becomes a fierce challenge, who flee from the drudgeries and hard responsibilities of life, who run out on life when it gets tough; in a society where escapism in all its corroding forms has become the moral atmosphere we breathe—we know what a magnificent triumph Jesus was.

II

Persevere with God's grace.

When we make decisions never to play the coward's role, never to give up, divine energies are released into our lives. But we are sustained in these efforts when our lives are deeply grounded in the spirit of Christ. Paul said, "Stand firm *in the Lord,* my beloved" (emphasis mine).

That's the secret. Hold on to the end—with God's power. In your decision not to quit on life but to hold on to the very end is released the power of eternity. To accept it, believe it, live in it—that's the meaning of standing firm in the Lord. Paul knew we cannot really hold out unless we believe our commitment to keep going has tied us into the Lord, into the reservoir of divine power.

If all I had to say to you in the face of life's hard and perplexing experiences was to try harder, fight the good fight, endure to the end, match yourself up to the life God wants you to live—if that were all that the Christian faith had to say—this would be a message of despair and not of hope.

But Christianity says we live in the Lord when we make a decision not to quit on life; we are put into a new relationship with the spiritual forces of the universe, so that we feel ourselves being lifted and carried to our fullest potential.

This spiritual paradox is at the very heart of human transformation. Without work and earnest effort no good will come our way, and yet nothing ever really comes to completion merely by trying! With penetrating insight Paul inextricably combines our efforts with God's grace: "You must work out your own salvation in fear and trembling; for it is God who works in you, inspiring both the will and the deed, for his own chosen purpose" (Phil. 2:12–13).

The moralist, the do-it-yourself religionist, says that we must change ourselves and lift ourselves up by our own bootstraps. But the gospel of Jesus says the success of changing ourselves lies both in our working at it and in our allowing Jesus to put us in a new relationship with the spiritual forces of the universe, so that we feel ourselves being changed and lifted up.

We have lots of fears, many things that burden our hearts. The strains are endless. But if we press the problem more intimately home, the thing each of us is really the most apprehensive about is ourself—and our own stamina and strength. Can we make it? Can we hold on to the end?

The gospel's message is that we *can* make it—by combining our work, persistence, tenacity, perseverance, and resolve with the limitless resources of God's power. Through our efforts God is at work in us to do God's will. God supports and sustains us in the long-distance run of life.

Do you know what the first major turning point was in the development of civilization? It has been said the great

moment came when someone planted a seed in the ground
and waited. Never before had women and men so cooperated
with the cosmic forces of the universe. They had tried to win
their way by their strong arms and iron wills, and without
that they would not have survived. But now a new era
dawned. Someone planted a seed in the ground and waited.
At that point began agriculture—and with it, civilization.
For at that point women and men began to relate themselves
creatively to the external forces of life and depend upon
them.

In this I see a parable about the spiritual life. We are
responsible for what we are becoming. Yet there is no great
attainment of our full potential without waiting, without
making some space for God to take hold of us. That is what
prayer is about—waiting patiently and expectantly for
God's power. Prayer is believing God wants us liberated
and made whole. Prayer is believing that a beautiful and
peace-filled life awaits us. Prayer is the courage to keep
searching in the confidence that God is at the rock bottom of
everything—every event, every person. Prayer is planting
the seed and taking time to remember all that, and hope all
that, and keep on hoping it until in its cosmic power a new
life is born.

III

I urge you to hang these pictures in the front room of your
mind.

Visualize those people you know who have not given up on
the world, who still believe it is possible to end hunger and
disease and human impoverishment, those who still give
themselves to the possibility of ending war forever.

Hold central in your mind those people you know who stand
up to life; who stay with it when the going is rough; who decide
that whatever else might happen, they just cannot see themselves running out on life; and who, in the mystery of the spirit
of God, know they are not alone—that the eternal power of
God holds them up and sustains them to the very end.

When Adlai Stevenson was Ambassador to the United Nations, he reported this on his return from a tour in Africa:

What impressed me most is the record of the missionaries there. Against every conceivable danger, it is they who brought education, and healing, and human caring to that continent. This was their legacy, and a trail of gravestones. My God, the gravestones, they were everywhere. It is as if they meant to say: "We are here to stay. We have come to help and be of good use to you. And we shall see it through."

Chapter Thirteen

Prayer: Flowing with the Tide of the Universe

Gerald Kennedy, one of the most colorful preachers of a generation ago, told of visiting the Bell Laboratories in California and seeing a most unusual gadget on the desk of an executive. It was a small wooden casket about the size of a cigar box. On one side of the box there was a single switch. When the executive flipped the switch, there was a buzzing sound, and the lid slowly rose. As it did, a mechanical hand emerged. Slowly, but surely, the hand reached down, turned off the switch, and went back in the box. Then the lid came down and the buzzing stopped.

That's all there was to it—a machine that did nothing but switch itself off!

I suspect that is a parable of life for some people. They wake up each morning and, machine-like, move through their daily routines then fall asleep again each night. Day after day they go through the same meaningless, monotonous motions, like the character in one of Ionesco's plays who says, "I'm exhausted from having done nothing with my life."

Carl Jung, in his book, *Modern Man in Search of a Soul,* makes this sobering statement: "About a third of my cases are suffering from no clinically definable neurosis, but from the senselessness and emptiness of their lives. . . ."[1]

God has made us for something better and more glorious than that, and somehow we know it and long for it. We seek a power that can bring authenticity, passion, vitality, and meaning to our lives.

Several years ago, when I was in Boston delivering some addresses, I went to the famous Union Oyster House for lunch. I sat right at the oyster bar, watching the man shuck the oysters. To this day I am surprised by what he said: "Yes, I've been shucking oysters here at the Union Oyster House for sixty-two years, and I've never had an oyster in my life."

"Not enough curiosity to try one?" I asked.

"Nope. Just never had one!"

I've been a minister in the church for thirty years, yet I continue to be surprised at the number of people who come to church but hang around the edges of the great power of the Christian experience. They're like that oyster shucker. They have come to church for years but have never come into the center of spiritual power and taken hold of it and let it invade their behavior.

You may be one of those people who urgently desires to come from the periphery to the center but does not know how. Engagement and growth in the power of the spirit is no easy task, but the rewards that await you are enormous.

One sure way to tap into that divine power is prayer. I want to admit quickly that prayer for me is a great mystery. I don't understand it fully, but then I don't fully understand the mystery of God! I must also admit that I don't understand how electricity works, either. But that has not prevented me from experiencing it—and depending on it.

Prayer is the way into the reservoir of divine power—I am profoundly convinced of that. And without that power the journey will be too difficult for us. Let me share with you some of my convictions about prayer. They may prove helpful to you.

I

Prayer is the conscious recognition of God dwelling deep within us.

The eternal Spirit dwells within you. God's energy is latent within your own spirit to work for your health, your pursuit of great dreams, your own inner transformation. Prayer is the conscious acceptance of that reality.

I remember the first time I saw Niagara Falls. The enormous power of that water was breathtaking and the amount of electricity generated, impressive. Yet the power is not *created* by the generators; rather, it is harnessed and appropriated.

So it is with God's power. Prayer does not create that divine power; it puts us in touch with the power that is within us, the power and energy given by the indwelling Spirit of God. Prayer is the conscious, intentional response to the gift of God's presence within us.

We must stop thinking of prayer as some method of persuading God to give us spiritual power or some way of getting God to change God's mind and overcome some divine reluctance. Prayer is not persuading God to act against God's will.

I remember that little girl who rushed home from school following a geography exam and looked hurriedly at a map. Then she dropped down on her knees and prayed, "O God, please quickly make Boston the capital of Vermont."

We chuckle at that prayer, but at last report God has not granted it. That's just not the way prayer works!

Prayer is putting ourselves close to the God of power so that God can do beautiful things in our lives. God's power dwells in us. We don't create it. We don't impose it. We simply open ourselves to the reality that is there. Our conscious acceptance of that gift releases God's energy in our lives.

Jesus said, "I am the vine, and you are the branches. He who dwells in me, as I dwell in him, bears much fruit; for apart from me you can do nothing" (John 15:5). To live in God's Spirit and bear fruit—healthy, beautiful, luscious fruit—that is prayer.

The God Jesus revealed is a God who wants life to be good, abundant, happy, healthy, peaceful. As parents want to give to their children, so God wants to give to those seeking a life of spiritual power. Prayer is our conscious recognition of this fact, and our hand reaching out to receive what God already wants us to have.

Sometimes that conscious response to God within us is made in solitude—when we are alone, thinking and pondering life, and say, "God, I'm yours." Sometimes we make that conscious response in the glorious worship of a congregation—when we say prayers together with other worshipers.

Either way, incredible things happen, for prayer puts us into union with the power that created us, the power in which our lives are grounded.

Jesus set no limit on the power of the Spirit of God. Astonishing things happen to people when they consciously and intentionally open themselves to that divine presence deep within them.

I've seen so many miracles when people united themselves to the spiritual power that is within them that I could never doubt its reality. I've seen men and women full of animosity toward everyone around them because they are so hostile toward themselves; men and women at the bottom of life, who were neither enjoying nor enhancing life; men and women in whose lives raged a violent storm; people whose bodies were full of sickness and whose minds pierced with pain because they were full of fear; men and women whose whole lives seemed like one continuous scene of defeat. And I've seen these people live again! I've seen them changed when they began to believe and trust in the goodness of God, when they gave themselves consciously through prayer to the divine power that dwelt within them.

I'm tempted to believe all transformation comes when we understand ourselves to be filled with God. That is grace.

Henri Nouwen, in his book, *Out of Solitude,* tells of a university professor going to a master to ask about Zen. The master served him tea. He poured his visitor's cup full, then kept pouring. The professor watched the overflow until he could no longer restrain himself. "It is over-full," he protested. "No more will go in!" "Like this cup," the master said, "you are full of your own opinions and speculations. How can I teach you Zen unless you first empty your cup?"[2]

The source of life's victory is grace, and we discover it when we empty ourselves and then let God fill us, when we consciously place ourselves in dependence on this greater power. That is the victory that can overcome the world.

I love that cartoon of the man praying beside his bed with the caption, "Is there some way you could help me, but make it look like I did it all myself?" Prayer is that conscious recognition of God's power deep within us—and our willingness to depend on it and to live in it. This acceptance releases the energy to live life fully and passionately.

We urgently seek the divine power. Look no further. The power is in you. The opportunity for new life is here—now.

We are like those sailors on an old sailing vessel that had been blown off her course along the coast of South America. The crew had lost all sense of time and place. They were anxiously hoping for some port, for their water was running low. Finally they saw another ship and they signaled for water. The answer came back, "Let down your buckets. You're in the mouth of the Amazon River. There is fresh water all around."

For those looking for something to give their lives some meaning, for those looking for something to take the oldness out of life and give it once again its fresh vigor and wonder, for those looking for something to keep them going in the struggles for peace and justice against an environment of violence and greed—this is the hour! God is present now in power, and God is in us. All we have to do is let down those buckets.

If we allow God to have God's way in our lives, allow God to love us and to collaborate with us—as God delights to do—then the end will be our renewal, our growing into our full stature, our becoming those beautiful, grace-filled, complete persons we long to be. God is in us to bring it to pass. But we must let it happen.

II

Prayer is the conscious recognition of God's presence in the world.

John Masefield's poetic drama, *The Trial of Jesus*, portrays Pilate's wife as deeply concerned about the crucifixion. A Roman soldier comes to report that he found the tomb of Jesus empty, and Pilate's wife asks in great excitement, "Do you believe he is dead?"

"No, Lady, I don't."

"Then where is he?" she asks.

"Loose in the world, Lady, where neither Jew nor Roman can stop his faith."[3]

Prayer is the recognition of the divine spirit let loose in the world. God is transcendent, beyond this created world. But God is also at the center of all things. As Robert Browning wrote, "Earth's crammed with heaven and every common bush afire with God." Prayer is the conscious recognition of that.

The account of Moses and the burning bush is one of the most moving stories in the Bible for me. I think this is because I'm guilty sometimes of seeking God on the splendid mountaintop of ecstasy and not realizing that I have passed God every step of the way up.

The Bible says that Moses, who was tending his father-in-law's sheep,

> led his flock to the west side of the wilderness, and came to Horeb, the mountain of God. And the angel of the Lord appeared to him in a flame of fire out of the midst of a bush; and he looked, and lo, the bush was burning, yet it was not consumed. And Moses said, "I will turn aside and see this great sight, why the bush is not burnt." When the Lord saw that he turned aside to see, God called to him out of the bush, "Moses, Moses!" And he said, "Here am I." Then he said, "Do not come near; put off your shoes from your feet, for the place on which you are standing is holy ground" (Exod. 3:1–5, RSV).

"Moses, Moses, put off your shoes from your feet, for the place on which you are standing is holy ground." At first it was just a bush—then suddenly it was on fire with the power of the Lord.

The real power of prayer comes when our eyes are opened and we see the world as God's miracle. The real power of prayer comes when we realize that we are surrounded on every side by miracles and are filled with awe and wonder that God dwells at the very center of life. This also means that the political, social, psychological worlds are God's arena. And only as we sense God's presence there do we experience the true power of prayer.

In the many years I have served as senior minister to the large institution of All Saints Church, with its complex structure, vast array of programs, and large staff, I have come to see the Spirit at work in so many ways.

I have come to see that the conference tables around which we sit and struggle, argue and laugh, cry and love are the altars of God—and the nuts and bolts of organizational management are the bread and wine of Eucharist. And sometimes I think I hear God speaking to me in those meetings, "George, George, take off your shoes, for the place where you are standing is holy ground."

The painting of the crucifixion that has meant the most to me over the years hangs on my study wall. It is Salvador Dali's modern reproduction of what has been called the "Christ of St. John of the Cross." It was sketched originally by a medieval monk. The painting shows a gap in the sky, and in that gap a cross above the earth. The cross is tilted so that the man on the cross can look down at our life on the earth. The wood of the cross is still there—and the nails—but the nails have gone clear through the wood into the very eternal ground and heart of reality.

I love the Salvador Dali cross, for it seems to say that this Christ of love over hatred and life over death is now part of the universe—the very nature of the universe—that this Christ is let loose and available to everything in creation.

I believe the way to tap into those spiritual resources for the journey is to see the Creator in the creation, to say again and again, "I believe in people; I believe in things—because God is in them." In a cup of coffee given to a street person who is in distress and confusion, we see the eternal dimensions of God who is the living water and bread of life.

The ordinary is the ground of the sacred. In a person who refuses to give up, who keeps on hoping when the lights go out, who loves in the midst of hatred, who forgives even the deepest hurts—in all that we see the human face of God. Prayer is the conscious recognition of God in all of life.

My experience would lead me to believe that the sacred, the holy, in its naked glory almost always eludes us. We don't see

God face to face until eternity. Here on the earth we see God only in the commonplace; we see the creator in the marvelous creation. We want to get connected with Christ, but the living Christ eludes us until finally we get connected to Christ's people, to our brothers and sisters in a church who are trying to live Christ's life. And then we find Christ in all his glory.

Richard J. Foster, in *Freedom of Simplicity,* gives focus to this thought: "Every person, every tree, every flower, every color is alive with God for those who know his language. Kagawa said that every scientific book was a letter from God telling us how he runs his universe."[4]

This conviction has expressed itself in a daily practice of mine: I pray as I read the newspaper or watch television or pass people on the streets of the city. Many years ago I read a book by Frank Laubach, the famous apostle of literacy, called, *Prayer: The Mightiest Force in the World,* in which he talked about cultivating this practice. He said he would bring his whole self into a quick prayer for someone he saw in a tough spot, as though his very body and nervous system were beaming power toward the person. So now I seldom read or hear of some tragedy that I don't say to myself, "God, strengthen those people for the task ahead."

Not long ago, on a Friday, I boarded an airplane in Chicago bound for Los Angeles. Sitting across the aisle from me was a young couple and a very tiny baby who was obviously their first child. I don't think I've ever heard a child scream as loudly and with as much determination as this child—except a few I've had in our church for baptism. And the father held the child tightly in his arms, literally punching a pacifier into the child's mouth. The man was so tense and the child so upset. The harder he tried to quiet the child, the louder the baby screamed.

I said somewhat selfishly but still sincerely, "God, please help that man relax; help him to hold that baby lightly; take all that tension from his arms." I had no sooner beamed my prayer toward him than he looked over at me. I smiled innocently. In a matter of minutes that baby was quiet and slept all the way to Los Angeles. And I worked on my sermon!

Say what you please about prayer and coincidence. I must answer with what Archbishop William Temple once said, "All I know is that when I stop praying the coincidences stop happening."

III

Prayer is the conscious effort to create a center of leisure inside of you.

In this overplanned, busy, harassing world, prayer means that we create a patient, unhurried time in which we can listen to the deepest things in life, to the most authentic person within us, to the urgings of the Spirit of God.

We live best when we live out of the richness of the Spirit; when we honor those quiet times alone; when we take time to ponder, brood, and pray. We live best when we are tuned in to the world of eternity and experience life at the center.

Thomas Kelly, in *Testament of Devotion*, writes, "We have hints that there is a way of life vastly richer and deeper than all this hurried existence, a life of unhurried serenity and peace and power. If only we could slip over into that Center!"[5]

Sometimes our consciences are out of condition, insensitive and lacking that unfailing moral compass; sometimes our minds are filled with prejudices, fears, and false reports; sometimes our imaginations are saturated with the vulgar and bleak stuff of life; sometimes our hearts are closed tight and we balk at doing the risky things that make for a new world; sometimes our wills are stubborn and selfish and refuse to be mastered so that we can become the servants of others. Then we tune in to the world of eternity; we push into the Center, the core—the divine presence. And when we do, incredible things happen, for we tap into the reservoirs of divine power.

Being the minister of a fast-moving, crazy, wonderful, chaotic, exciting, challenging parish is a hard job, and I love it intensely. But I do better in this job when I take care of myself. I didn't learn that in seminary, but it became clear to me at a very early time in the priesthood that unless I took care of my own spiritual life—my own deep places—I got into real trouble.

Some graffiti I saw some years ago sticks in my mind: "Don't just do something; stand there." Precisely! What a gigantic struggle it has been in my overactivated, hyperthyroid ministry to hold sacred and inviolable those hours in my study, away from people, telephones, and colleagues.

I have a ministry to myself. I must provide time and space where I can listen to the deepest things in life and to the Spirit of God at work within me; where I can pray and struggle; where I can study with the passion of a lover for his beloved; where in all of this I am fed, so that I have something to offer to my people. I do not let people take that time from me—or, if I do let them, I feel it is the work of the devil and I have failed my people.

All Saints Church is a magnanimous congregation to serve—so responsive to my work, so supportive of my aspirations, so candid but gentle in its criticism. But there have been some struggles.

I remember a time when some members of my church vigorously objected to my efforts to stop the Vietnam war. Many opposed my peace work honorably, and they are still among my best friends. But others were vicious in their opposition. After one harsh, acrimonious evening with a group of such people who attacked my ministry, questioned my integrity, and wanted my termination as rector because of my views on the escalating war, I remember going home a deeply shaken and depressed person.

I stayed up most of the night thinking and pondering and praying. Over and over I kept repeating Psalm 27: "Wait for the Lord; be strong, take courage, and wait for the Lord" (v. 14). Through that dark and lonely night I prayed and paced. Toward morning, from the deep recesses of my spirit, there came to my conscious mind that powerful verse from 2 Chronicles 20:12: "O God our God . . . we know not what we ought to do; we lift our eyes to thee." That day I returned to the office refreshed and made my way once more through those turbulent waters.

Robert Frost, in one of his poems, tells of how many bolts of lightning it required before Benjamin Franklin took the hint and how many apples had to fall before Newton took the hint. Frost encourages us to realize that hints are perpetually being given, but only the open and attentive person gets the message, and only the unpreoccupied person responds to the hint.

God wants to get through to our hearts and minds; God wants to get through to this misdirected world. But in our haste those hints go unnoticed—or, if they *are* noticed, they go unheeded.

Of course, hindsight is always clearer than foresight—but most of us know our foresight could be better than it is. This malady affects most of us. We act without thinking; we speak without considering; we push ahead without planning; we move quickly without praying—and we suffer for it. The hints are given, but without a center of leisure inside of us they go by unnoticed.

Life is busy and demanding. I wouldn't change that fact even if I could. But the only way I know for my life to bear fruit that is lovely and delicious is for me to be willing to listen unhurriedly to what God is saying to me.

That has never been easy for me. As Dag Hammarskjöld said in *Markings,* "The longest journey is the journey inward."[6] But it is probably the most important journey of our lives.

Down in that inward journey, in those quiet centers of leisure, where the volume of the world's stereo has been turned down, we hear the plaintive cry of our spirits as we look at the monumental achievements of our age: Is that all that there is to life? What does it profit us to gain the whole world and lose our soul?

And we hear in those deep places the voice of Jesus, which we ignore at our great peril: I am the vine and you are the branches. Dwell in me and bear much fruit. If you don't dwell in me you will wither away.

IV

Prayer is consciously striving to live congruently with the purposes of God.

Prayer can be verbal, it can be mental, or it can be active. But all praying is our response to God in the Center—the core of our being—as well as our participation as a co-creator with God in the midst of secular life.

When we pray, we become a source of unity rather than estrangement in the universe. When we pray, we accept the responsibility of being co-creator with God. When we pray, we open the channel to receive the power for a new creation. When we pray, we flow with the tide of the cosmos; we align our lives with the grain of the universe.

When we look at prayer through these lenses, it comes alive with power and integrity. So we strive to live congruently with the purposes of God. That conscious decision releases into our lives the energy of the God of creation.

What are the purposes of God? Come with me to the Upper Room following the crucifixion of Jesus. It is late Sunday evening. The disciples, who had deserted Jesus in his hour of ignominy and abuse as he suffered on the cross, are huddled behind locked doors for fear of the authorities. Then the risen Christ comes and stands among them.

"Peace be with you!" he says. "As the Father sent me, so I send you." Then he breathes on them, saying, "Receive the Holy Spirit!" (John 20:19–22).

"As God sent me—" Jesus was saying, "sent me first to love the unlovable and endure hatred with mercy and bring peace to a divided world; as God sent me to embody goodness, gentleness, gladness before the old world and die for it all rather than submit to the little gods of the earth—so I send you. You are my arms of healing mercy. You are my heart of compassionate love. I send you in my name."

Look specifically at what, I believe, it means to pray with our lives:

When we struggle to see a piece of legislation passed that will protect the elderly and give them medical care with dignity—that is prayer.

When we work for quality integrated education, good education for black and white and Latino children in the inner city—that is prayer.

When we strive to change the direction of the spiraling arms race and preserve the planet and enhance it—that is prayer.

When we open ourselves in trust to the healing powers of the universe and continue to hope for life—that is prayer.

When we reach a hand across a chasm of estrangement and seek reconciliation—that is prayer.

When we offer compassion and warmth to a stranger who is intimidated by a crowd of people—that is prayer.

When we visit in a convalescent home and bring friendship and joy into a bleak environment—that is prayer.

When we do these things, we are responding to the divine presence. God is in the midst of life.

Abraham Heschel has written many things on prayer that have directed and enriched my thinking. He once said, "When I marched in Selma with Martin Luther King, Jr., I felt my legs were praying."

The authentic mark of the Spirit of God in a church is when that church is sent out in mission and boldly puts its words into action.

I remember a man seated in my office some years ago who wanted to make a deal. He promised to make a significant amount of money available to All Saints Church's ministry if I promised not to speak again about "political things" from the pulpit. And this is what "politics from the pulpit" was for my friend, the issues being addressed which he thought inappropriate: the savagery of war and militarism that pervaded our culture; the struggle of our minority brothers and sisters to have power to determine their own destinies; the despair of the unemployed and the absence of federal funds to aid the unemployable; the need for quality, integrated public schools; the grossly distorted priorities of our nation which spends more and more on arms and less and less on the poor and hungry and sick.

In my mind, that man's request was really a request for us to ignore the Holy Spirit. For I believe with all my heart that we are called to be involved in the issues that affect the well-being of God's people and the future of God's creation. God will forgive our failures—and at times we *will* fail. But God will be grieved by our unwillingness to go out and risk for the creation of a new world of peace and justice. That thwarts the power of the Holy Spirit, who wants to work through us.

As I have said often in this book, "You are somebody; you are important; you are of unique worth." Now it is crucial that you see that you are essential to the life-giving work God is calling us to do.

At the end of World War II, a couple of American GIs were helping some Italians rebuild a small village church destroyed by artillery fire. In the rubble they uncovered a statue of Christ. It was unharmed, except that its outstretched hands were gone.

"Shall we discard this statue?" the soldiers asked the priest.

"No," he said, "let's place it inside the church door for all to see as they enter and leave. It will remind us that Jesus has no other hands than ours."

Meister Eckhart, the thirteenth-century German mystic, put it with unusual boldness: "God can as little do without us, as we without him." That is not arrogant boasting, but a statement of high responsibility. We are essential instruments in the fulfillment of the eternal purpose of God.

One evening a couple of years ago, I went to a fancy, high-priced banquet in Beverly Hills. I had one purpose in mind. Archbishop Desmond Tutu of South Africa was being honored, and I wanted to see him, touch him, hug him, and tell him we loved him and were praying for him. He laughed and said it wasn't worth the money to come and see him but he was glad I came.

Later, in his magnificent speech at the Beverly Hilton Hotel's International Ballroom, Archbishop Tutu said something that still rings in my ears: "The great God of the cosmos, the great creator God, the God that holds the whole creation in his hands and guides it to its fulfillment—that God says, 'I need you. Please help me! I need you to transform the hatred of this world so that blacks and whites can hold hands together. I need you. Please help me!'"

You are important. You are somebody. You are of unique worth. You are essential to the fulfillment of the eternal purpose of God.

One day a woman stood in the midst of a group of starving children in Ethiopia, their bodies ravaged with hunger, their fearful eyes bulging from their listless faces. She said she wanted to scream out at God until she realized that God was screaming at her.

God has entrusted us—you and me—with the responsibility and the glorious privilege of carrying out Christ's mission. We are co-creators. We are partners with God. That is how God has chosen to work. Jesus has no other arms than ours. "As God sent me, so I send you."

We who seek to tap into the reservoir of divine power need to come up close to a central truth of the New Testament. God doesn't waste power. God's power is released in those who tackle something so great, so overwhelming, that their own resources are insufficient.

Paul Tillich once said, "To be alive is to have a center around which life's energies are focused, and toward which they are directed."

A life full of power has nothing to do with years—nothing. It has to do with a sense of purpose and the meaning we attach to what we are doing and how well we are doing it. It has to do with our dreams and what we allow to happen to those dreams.

Powerful, passionate, vital life belongs to those who somehow grasp or are grasped by a dream, an overarching purpose, larger than they are. Some find it at fifteen and others at seventy. But find it we must if we are to live with power.

When a desperately sick man who had tried to assassinate President Franklin Roosevelt was asked if he belonged to a church, he cried, "No! No! I belong to nothing! I belong only to myself, and I suffer."

A life of power is found in giving your life away, remaining hopeful that the world is worth that gift, and not giving up on yourself and this creation.

I was talking to a woman at a party. She works among the

sick in the most impoverished parts of Los Angeles. I like this woman very much; we've always been close. But she jolted me with her pessimism. She chronicled all the tragic things happening in America to the poor and contributing to the disintegration of our corporate health as a nation. And she stated flatly, "I just don't have any hope things will change. There is nothing left in me but despair."

This woman didn't like it when I said that I thought her despair was quite a luxury in our age and that she would pay heavily for it personally. But I saw her a few months ago, and she looked as if she had aged ten years.

It's a hard world. It's no place for the cynic. Powerful life belongs to those whose hearts are caught up in the dreams of a better life and a better world.

To be alive is to have a center around which life's energies are focused. For me, that center is the wild dreams put forth by the biblical message:

- a people liberated from all the tyrannies that keep them from being whole;
- a land of beauty and loveliness;
- a society where none is afraid, and all are free to be who they are;
- a spiritual community in which God's power dwells and human personalities can be radically transformed;
- a human family where the needs of all are met, none hunger for food, sickness is tended, and jobs belong to all;
- a world community where war and the preparation for war in all its insanity and death are renounced forever.

I believe that when we take a step toward those wild, magnificent dreams of the Bible, God's power is released in us. God joins us in the struggle. The energy of creation is at our backs pushing us into the light.

V

I challenge you to pray again. When you do, great things will happen in your life and in the life of the world.

It is said that Voltaire was walking with a friend one day

when they passed a religious procession making its way down the street. At the sight of the cross, the agnostic Voltaire removed his hat and bowed his head.

The friend smiled at this irony. "I wasn't aware you knew God."

"Oh, you wouldn't call it knowing each other," Voltaire replied. "We nod to each other but we never speak."

I fear that characterizes so much of contemporary religion. We've given up on a commitment to a praying life. We nod but we don't speak. And we miss such glorious, passionate, vital life.

Start praying again today. Create that center of leisure and push forward to the core of divine energy. Listen to the deepest things in your being, and allow God to speak to your life with power and new perspective. Give yourself to a task too great for you, and allow God to sustain you. Affirm your solidarity with God's people—your brothers and sisters everywhere.

Such a life would put us on the way to passionate, authentic life. And the rewards are great: a conscience at peace when the shadows of evening lengthen and the busy world is hushed; a life made clean by frequent prayer and worship; a life made strong by the high resolve to reach out in love to the whole human family; a life with compassion's springs kept warm and vital and ready to give of one's resources for the needy of the world; a life of integrity which is obedient to the ideals of love and service, which brood over our earthly journey like a galaxy of stars; a life of companionship with Jesus, whose deep love forgives our mistakes and failures and claims us as sons and daughters.

That is wealth beyond all price. It is the treasure within, the treasure the world cannot give or ever take away.

Notes

Introduction

1. Rollo May, *Love and Will* (New York: W. W. Norton & Co., 1969), p. 43.

Chapter One

1. Frederick Buechner, *The Sacred Journey* (San Francisco: Harper & Row Pubs., 1982), p. 61.

Chapter Two

1. Maya Angelou, *All God's Children Need Traveling Shoes* (New York: Random House, 1986), p. 207, emphasis added.
2. Martin Luther King, Jr., "A Testament of Hope," in *The Essential Writings of Martin Luther King, Jr.,* ed. James M. Washington (San Francisco: Harper & Row Pubs., 1986), pp. 219–220.

Chapter Three

1. John Van Druten, *I Remember Mama,* in *Eight American Ethnic Plays,* ed. Francis Griffith and Joseph Mersand (New York: Charles Scribner's Sons, 1974), pp. 120–121.

Chapter Four

1. John A. Redhead, *Getting to Know God* (Nashville: Abingdon Press, 1954), pp. 110–111.
2. Bruce Larson, *There's a Lot More to Health Than Not Being Sick* (Waco, Tex.: Word Books, 1981), p. 142.

Chapter Five

1. Herman Wouk, *The Caine Mutiny* (Garden City, N.Y.: Doubleday & Co., 1951), p. 457.
2. Harold Kushner, *When All You've Ever Wanted Isn't Enough* (New York: Summit Books, 1986), p. 158.
3. Quoted by Rollo May, *Love and Will* (New York: W. W. Norton & Co., 1969), p. 102.

4. Bernard Levin, "In Praise of Exuberance," *New York Times Magazine*, 15 April 1984, p. 51.

5. Lewis Smedes, *How Can It Be All Right When Everything Is All Wrong?* (San Francisco: Harper & Row Pubs., 1982), p. 33.

6. William Walsham How (1823–1897), "For All the Saints," *The Episcopal Church Hymnal 1982* (New York: Church Hymnal Corporation, 1985), no. 284.

Chapter Six

1. Alvin Toffler, *The Third Wave* (New York: William Morrow & Co., 1980), p. 384.

2. Robert Raines, *To Kiss the Joy* (Waco, Tex.: Word Books, 1973), p. 53.

3. Loren Eiseley, *The Immense Journey* (New York: Random House, 1970), p. 19.

4. Maya Angelou, *I Know Why the Caged Bird Sings* (New York: Random House, 1970), p. 19.

Chapter Seven

1. F. J. Foakes Jackson, *The Acts of the Apostles* (London: Hodder and Stoughton, 1931), p. 100.

2. Dag Hammarskjöld, *Markings* (New York: Alfred A. Knopf, 1964), p. 122.

3. Charles Swindoll, *Strengthening Your Grip* (Waco, Tex.: Word Books, 1982), pp. 99–100.

4. François Mauriac, *What I Believe* (New York: Farrar, Strauss & Giroux, 1963), p. 54.

Chapter Eight

1. Edward Fitzgerald, *The Rubaiyat of Omar Khayyam*, Edition 4.

2. Lewis Smedes, *How Can It Be All Right When Everything Is All Wrong?* (San Francisco: Harper & Row Pubs., 1982), p. 30.

3. Lewis Smedes, *Forgive and Forget* (New York: Pocket Books, 1984), p. 11.

4. Morton Thompson, *Not As a Stranger* (New York: Charles Scribner's Sons, 1954), p. 886.

Chapter Nine

1. Thornton Wilder, *Our Town* (San Francisco: Harper & Row Pubs., 1938), p. 100.

2. Arthur Miller, *The Death of a Salesman* (New York: Penguin Books, 1949), p. 137.

Chapter Ten

1. Walker Percy, *Lost in the Cosmos* (New York: Farrar, Strauss & Giroux, 1983), p. 1.
2. Arthur Miller, *After the Fall* (New York: Viking Press, 1964), p. 22.

Chapter Eleven

1. Morris West, *The Clowns of God* (New York: William Morrow & Co., 1981), p. 42.

Chapter Twelve

1. Robert Raines, *To Kiss the Joy* (Waco, Tex.: Word Books, 1973), p. 26.

Chapter Thirteen

1. Carl G. Jung, *Modern Man in Search of a Soul* (New York: Harcourt, Brace & Co., 1933), p. 20.
2. Henri Nouwen, *Out of Solitude* (Notre Dame, Ind.: Ave Maria Press, 1974), p. 42.
3. John Masefield, *The Trial of Jesus* (New York: Macmillan Publishing Co., 1925), p. 111.
4. Richard J. Foster, *Freedom of Simplicity* (San Francisco: Harper & Row Pubs., 1981), p. 85.
5. Thomas Kelly, *Testament of Devotion* (New York: Harper & Row Pubs., 1941), p. 115.
6. Dag Hammarskjöld, *Markings* (New York: Alfred A. Knopf, 1964), p. 58.